Gary D.

D0390232

WHAT WE KNOW ABOUT JESUS

WHAT WE KNOW
ABOUT JESUS

Stephen Neill

WILLIAM B. EERDMANS PUBLISHING COMPANY
GRAND RAPIDS, MICHIGAN

First published 1970 by Lutterworth Press, London, England.
Sponsored by the Commission on World Mission and Evangelism of the World Council of Churches.

First American edition published by arrangement with Lutterworth Press, June 1972

Library of Congress Catalog Card No.: 72-75569

ISBN 0-8028-1473-5

Printed in the United States of America

Reprinted, November 1973

CONTENTS

The Scripture quotations in this book are from the Revised Standard Version of the Bible.

CHAPTER ONE

THERE REALLY IS A PROBLEM

How much do we know for certain about Jesus of Nazareth?

The answers that are given to this question in the modern world are quite astonishingly varied. It will help us to focus the problem, if we state simply the two extreme views.

1. Some learned men have set themselves to show that Jesus never really lived at all. According to this view, a number of eagerly religious people in what we call the first century A.D. joined together, in their own over-heated imaginations, a number of myths about a divine redeemer which were current in the world of their time. Out of their confident hope that God was going to intervene to save the world they developed the belief that God had already so intervened. This belief clothed itself in the figure of a man who had never really existed at all, but to whom they gave the mythological name "Saviour", in Aramaic Jesus (Joshua) a common name among Palestinian Jews of that time. According to this theory, then, the Gospel story had its origin in imagination and not in fact.

2. At the other extreme, pious Christians, finding in their New Testament four Gospels, have read these books with the deepest veneration, believing that every word is divinely inspired, and an authentic witness to the Son of God who came and lived among men for their salvation. It is inconvenient that the Gospels do not perfectly agree with one another. The reader can verify this by comparing the accounts in the various Gospels of the healing of the paralysed man who was brought

into the presence of Jesus by four of his friends (Matt. 9: 1–8; Mark 2: 1–12; Luke 5: 17–26). Indeed it is enough to compare the lists given in the New Testament of the names of the twelve disciples of Jesus, none of which exactly agrees with any other (Matt. 10: 2–4; Mark 3: 16–19; Luke 6: 14–16; Acts 1: 13). The old-fashioned believer is not disturbed by any of these difficulties. He is convinced that in the light of careful study these differences will simply disappear; in point of fact very ingenious solutions—sometimes more ingenious than convincing—have been put forward for all these difficulties.

The unprejudiced student may think that we are likely to find the solution to our problem somewhere between the two extremes.

It really requires a good deal of credulity to believe that Jesus never existed. It is true that we have no contemporary evidence, outside the New Testament, about him, and that what we have from Roman writers in the next century or two is rather thin. But these few passages from Tacitus, Suetonius and Josephus show clearly that the Romans, who were a hard-headed people, were convinced that the man Jesus had existed in Judaea and had been crucified. Moreover, it is not easy to believe that, within fifty years after the date at which he was supposed to have died, so large a volume of literature—half the New Testament at least—had been composed about someone who had never really existed. The strongest argument of all, however, is the early existence of the Christian movement. By the year A.D. 112 it had become so strong as to cause considerable anxiety to Pliny, the Roman governor of Bithynia. Movements live by ideas; but we understand today, as historians did not always understand in the past, that behind every great movement stands some remarkable personality. Without someone like Jesus Christ as he is depicted in the Gospels, the Christian movement could not possibly have come into existence.

What, then, is the historical value of the Gospels? Critics draw attention to the length of time that elapsed between the death of Jesus and the composition of the first Gospel—at least thirty years, and perhaps as much as forty. Many people today are dimly aware that the earliest manuscripts of the New Testament that we possess are from the third century; they are disturbed by their awareness of this long period in which, as they imagine, all kinds of corruptions or inventions could have crept in. If we hold, as many devout Christians do, that the evangelists were miraculously preserved from every kind of error, the interval between fact and record will not cause us the slightest distress. But if, like many other equally devout Christians, we are prepared to recognize that there is a human element in the writings of the New Testament, that human memories are fallible, and that even the most scrupulous observers find it hard to record things exactly as they happened, we may find it difficult to rely simply on a doctrine of inspiration as the answer to all our questions.

If we are Christians, the aim of all our questioning is to come nearer to the Lord in whom we believe. Obviously the Gospels must be a primary source. But we are entitled to ask whether we can, as it were, look back through the Gospels and find out what was happening in the period between the life of Jesus and the writing down of the Gospel stories.

Part of the answer to this question soon becomes clear. Because the Gospels come at the beginning of all our New Testaments, most readers tend to assume without question that this was the first part of the New Testament to be written. But, in point of fact, this is not so. It is probable that all the Epistles of Paul, and perhaps some other parts of the New Testament as well, were in existence before ever the earliest Gospel was written down. If we read the Epistles with attention, they will tell us a great deal about what these early Christians believed about Jesus before the Gospels were written.

Secondly we can come to the Gospels themselves with new questions. Many scholars are convinced that, by asking the right questions, we can work back from the Gospels to the period in which little or nothing had been written down and in which the faith of the earliest disciples was being formed; and then from that earliest faith to the Person whose life and death had brought that faith into being. If the enterprise of questioning brings us nearer to Jesus of Nazareth as he was, and to that explosion of divine power in which the Church of Christ had its origin, surely the enterprise will have been worth while.

Some will be inclined to answer, "Is not this the wrong way of going about it? Must we not start with the acceptance of faith? And if we have believed in Jesus, shall we not find in him entirely satisfactory answers to all our questions? Then will not any solutions that can be offered by theology and historical criticism seem to be irrelevant, or at best no more then interesting footnotes to a text which itself is all-important?"

This is an argument which cannot simply be disregarded. One point we shall readily concede. If it were possible for historical research to demonstrate beyond all possibility of doubting that everything in the Gospels happened exactly as it is recorded, that Jesus spoke every word exactly as the evangelist wrote it down, and that he made exactly the claims that he is alleged to have made, all this together would not avail to produce what Christians have always understood by faith. Faith does not mean accepting as a historical fact that Jesus was like this or that; it means that Jesus is this or that *for me*; and that, this being so, Jesus presents me with a challenge to which I must answer decisively Yes or No.

What, on the other hand, would be our situation, if research could prove conclusively that Jesus as he really was did not in the least resemble Jesus as he is presented to us in the Gospels? Let us suppose, to take an extreme case, that the body of Jesus of Nazareth were to be discovered in such a manner as to make it impossible that he could have risen from the dead in any way corresponding to what is recorded in the Gospels? What, then, would happen to the faith of the Church? Or, if it could be shown, as some scholars think, that St. John's Gospel gives us the pious reflections of a third-generation believer on the life of Jesus, *and nothing more*, how can we use that Gospel to strengthen and to clarify our faith?

Some Christians never want to ask such questions, and are not interested in the fact that these questions are being very widely debated both inside and outside the Church. But we cannot forbid the asking of the questions, and we ought not to condemn as unbelievers those who feel compelled by honesty to ask them. A historical question is in search of a historical answer, and will not be stilled by an appeal to faith. The fact that a question is asked does not mean that it will necessarily be possible to answer it. In the field of history what is offered us is usually no more than probability, a poor substitute in the eyes of many for the certainty which faith seeks. Yet Christian faith rightly claims to have its roots in history. Therefore historical research must have its place in relation to that faith.

We must be careful in our use of historical method. The questions must be rightly formulated. We must be scrupulously careful to make use of all the evidence that there is. We must do our best to keep our own prejudices and preferences under control. We must not stretch the evidence further than it will go; but equally we must not try to invalidate evidence that does not fit in with our preconceptions. We must not be unduly disturbed, if at times we put forward questions to which no reliable answer can be given.

11

Some will feel that the application of such methods to the story of Jesus of Nazareth is too dangerous. A few scholars have, indeed, laid such violent hands on the Gospels, and have used such methods, that at the end of their work hardly anything is left of Jesus of Nazareth, and that what remains seems hardly sufficient to account for the birth of the Christian Church, and of the influence that it has exercised over nineteen centuries. But this is not the necessary result of historical research. Almost all who have engaged in it have found that their understanding of Jesus has been changed; some parts of their faith have been tested, have been found inadequate, and have had to be cast away. At the same time, however, the result for many has been that Jesus has been seen as far more human, real, and winning than he had been allowed to appear in many of the traditions of the Church. Need he for that reason be less majestic, less commanding, less qualified to be the sovereign of our hearts?

It is the New Testament itself which tells us that "There is one God, and one mediator between God and men, *the man Christ Jesus*" (1 Tim. 2: 5).

CHAPTER TWO

THE DISCIPLES

For all that we know of Jesus Christ we are indebted to his disciples. No disciples, no Christian Church—this statement is hardly an exaggeration. It will, therefore, be sensible to start our enquiry with the disciples and with what we can learn about them from the sources at our disposal. The only direct accounts we have of the disciples are to be found in the Gospels and in the Acts of the Apostles; but from other sources we can learn a good deal of their background, of the communities from which they came and of the way in which their minds had been conditioned by earlier beliefs. All this would certainly affect the way in which they would react to Jesus Christ, and the manner in which they would adapt what they learned of him to their own way of thinking.

Jesus, during his ministry, was constantly surrounded by crowds of people—on this all our sources are agreed. Gradually more intimate groups began to disentangle themselves from the crowd; the central group came to be known as "The Twelve". After the death of Jesus "The Twelve" played an important part in bearing witness to that faith out of which in course of time the Christian Church developed.

We can state one or two things about this central group with almost complete certainty. They were all men, though the records suggest that a large number among the intimate followers of Jesus were women. They were all Jews.

But this statement that all were Jews lacks precision. We know a good deal, from sources outside the New Testament, about the state of the Jewish people in the first century; we find that there was among them a great variety of conviction and practice.

1. The discovery of the now famous Dead Sea Scrolls has revealed to us a form of Judaism of which previously we knew very little. These ancient scrolls written in the Hebrew language have brought to light for us a monastic community living at Qumran in the neighbourhood of the Dead Sea. The majority of the scholars who have wrestled with the problems of the Scrolls are of the opinion that we here have to do with the people called Essenes, about whom we do have some information in the works of the Jewish writers Philo and Josephus. They had developed for themselves a strict rule of life, marked by a number of ascetic practices. They looked back to the foundation of their sect, probably about 100 B.C., by one whom they called the Teacher of Righteousness. They thought in terms of war between the "sons of light" and "the sons of darkness", and they looked for the coming of a Messiah (in some documents two Messiahs) who would establish righteousness upon earth in the name of the Lord. It is not clear that this community exercised much influence on the minds of their fellow-Jews who were not members of the sect. Some scholars think, however, that John the Baptist had been influenced by this teaching and may even have been a member of the Qumran community.

2. On the left wing of main-line Judaism stood the Zealots. They represented rather a point of view and an attitude than a system of doctrine. They hated bitterly the Gentile and idolatrous power which had usurped control over Israel. To overthrow the Roman power they were prepared to use every weapon of force and of rebellion. They were responsible for the outbreaks of violence, which continually disturbed the tranquillity of Roman rule, and one of which seems to have taken place in the week in which Jesus was condemned to

14

death. Barabbas was not an ordinary robber; he had been put in prison for "an insurrection started in the city, and for murder" (Luke 23: 19; cf. Mark 15: 7). In the dark years after the death of Jesus, the influence of these extremists continued to grow, until in A.D. 66 the nation embarked on the fatal and hopeless war against the Romans, which ended with the destruction of Jerusalem in A.D. 70.

3. Less violent than the Zealots, though not wholly unsympathetic to their aims, were the Pharisees, whom we constantly meet in the pages of the Gospels. They seem to have been the successors of the *Hasidim*, "the righteous ones", who, in the days of persecution, in which Antiochus Epiphanes (175–163 B.C.) wished to overthrow the Jewish religion, stood for the integrity of the faith, and for obedience to the Law of God. The Pharisees have been given a bad name as narrow and self-righteous people, concerned about the minute details of legal observance and inclined to lose their sense of proportion in matters of religion. We ought not to forget the other side; they genuinely loved the law of God, and there was among them a strain of deep and sincere piety.

4. At the centre stood those who were sometimes known as "the quiet in the land", who could not be identified with any group or party, who valued the worship of the Temple, tried to live in conformity with God's law, and devoutly believed that one day God would intervene to save his people. They did not believe that men ought to attempt to bring that day nearer. The first two chapters of Luke's Gospel give a beautiful picture of this loose fellowship, to which Simeon and Anna belonged, and in which the family of Jesus seems to have felt itself at home.

5. The most powerful party among the Jews was undoubtedly that of the Sadducees. Theologically this was the conservative party; they held to the Law as the most sacred part of the Old Testament, and did not admit such ideas as that of

the resurrection, which had come into Judaism only at the end of the Old Testament period. The aristocratic families in Jerusalem belonged to this group, and made a good thing out of their control of the Temple, of its sacrifices and of the tax which had to be paid to it by every Jew. Moreover, they had succeeded in making a pact with the Romans, under which they wielded considerable power in the internal affairs of the nation. In return they undertook to see that the Roman authority was not seriously challenged. A party of this kind is certain to be moderate in everything—too much religion leads to fanaticism, and too much liberty leads to democratic chaos.

6. The Herodians were more a political than a religious party. The Herods were not Jews at all but Edomites. Disliked and distrusted by the majority of Jews, they had succeeded in acquiring great influence, and at times large tracts of territory to rule, by their personal friendship with the imperial family in Rome, and by their dexterity in working out a kind of compromise between Jewish religion and Greek culture. They would have maintained that they still held the faith of the God of Israel, but believed that Israel could not keep itself isolated from the wider currents of the life of the world.

When there was so great variety among the Jews, is it possible to speak at all of a common Jewish faith? It certainly is possible. On some vital matters, which radically distinguished them from all other people, all Jews were at one:

1. They believed most firmly that God had chosen them to be his people among all the peoples of the world, and that his special relationship to them could best be described by the word "Covenant".

2. They held that Israel's share in the covenant was to be obedience, and that an essential part of this obedience was the rite of circumcision.

16

3. They believed that Israel's depressed state at the time at which they were living was due to disobedience on the part of the people in the past.

4. They looked forward to a day of deliverance in which God would interfere on their behalf through his "Messiah", though they differed widely in their understanding of how this deliverance would take place.

5. They expected, with the prophets of the Old Testament (Isaiah 2: 2–3; Zech. 8: 20–23), that Jerusalem the holy city would become the centre of the world to which all nations would come to receive the Law of the Lord.

So much unity we can readily recognize. But we must here pause to look at another deep division of opinion, which did not exactly correspond to the division of parties, but ran through all parties in relation to their expectations of the future. The division can be expressed in terms of the difference between "prophecy" and "apocalyptic".

The prophet spoke directly into a historical situation. He saw his people threatened by an identifiable human enemy—e.g., "the fierce anger of Rezin and Syria, and of the son of Remaliah" (Isaiah 7: 4). If the Lord promises deliverance, that will take place upon this earthly theatre; in certain cases the name of the deliverer is given—"Thus says the Lord to his anointed, to Cyrus, whose right hand I have grasped, to subdue nations before him" (Isaiah 45: 1). Apocalyptic, on the other hand, developed as the hopes of any human deliverance failed. The enemies are now seen as gigantic cosmic powers; the redemption of God's people can take place only through worldwide destruction, and the introduction of a new order, a new world. In the Old Testament there is one great Apocalypse, Daniel 7–12, in which the powers of the world are seen under the form of savage beasts, whose dominion in the end is to be replaced by the kingdom which God will give to one like the Son of man (Daniel 7: 13). Such language is familiar to us from the New Testament also: "In those days . . . the sun will be darkened, and the moon will not give its light. And the stars will be falling from heaven, and the powers in the heavens will be shaken" (Mark 13: 24–25). This is the language of apocalypse and not of prophecy.

Many such apocalypses were in circulation among certain circles among the Jews. One of the most remarkable of these is the Book of Enoch (referred to in Jude 14). Here we find in a number of passages a figure called "the Son of Man", who has been hidden from the beginning, but at the end of the days will appear to do judgement.

And the sum of judgment was given unto the Son of Man,
  And he caused the sinners to pass away and be destroyed . . .
For that Son of Man has appeared,
  And has seated himself on the throne of his glory.

(Enoch 69: 27–29)

Here we find obvious parallels to New Testament language. Is it probable that books such as the Book of Enoch were being circulated and read in circles to which people like Jesus and his disciples may have belonged? To this we can give no certain answers. All we can say is that apocalyptic ideas were fairly widely disseminated among the Jews at that time, and that these ideas are likely to have influenced the minds of many people who had never read any of the books in which they were actually set out in written form.

So much for the background of the disciples in the life of Palestine in the period in which they lived. For all this we have fairly reliable authority in Jewish writings outside the New Testament. For more direct information about the disciples themselves we have hardly any source other than the New Testament itself. We shall proceed cautiously, asking what general impression we can form of the disciples, taking the New Testament evidence as a whole.

It seems clear that none of them belonged to the learned or

scholarly class. Matthew, who is described as having been a tax-gatherer, was probably better educated than the rest. This, however, by no means indicates that they were a set of ignorant countrymen. The Jews had a great tradition of education. The synagogue, in which the sacred scrolls of the Scriptures were preserved, was the centre of the life of the scattered communities. Here the growing boy, apart from hearing these Scriptures regularly read and expounded week by week in the Sabbath services, would have the opportunity to learn to read and understand the ancient Hebrew, which, since it had been replaced by the kindred Aramaic, was no longer currently spoken. This may be thought a narrow kind of education. But exposure to the great ideas and words of the Scripture in itself produces a noble enlargement of the mind, and can result in a high level of culture. It was from such a level of society that Jesus and his friends were drawn.

Of only one of these disciples are we told that he belonged to one particular group. In Luke 6: 15 the second Simon is described as having the additional title "Zelotes", the Zealot (Matthew and Mark, "the Cananaean"); this seems certainly to imply that he belonged or had belonged to the extreme group of the Zealots. Several of the others seem to have come under the influence of John the Baptist (John 1: 29–42) whose earnest preaching of moral reformation as a preparation for an imminent intervention of God in the life of his people had caused no small stir among the Jews. This suggests that they were among those who were eagerly expecting the deliverance of Israel, though it is not possible to be more precise as to the exact opinions they may have held as to what the nature of the deliverance would be.

Some among them may have felt some sympathy for the Pharisees. The reality of religious faith among the best of the Pharisees would be likely to attract young men to whom the worldliness of the Sadducees would make no appeal. Indeed, it is at least possible that, when Jesus began to preach, his deep demand for sincerity, and his uncompromising insistence on the moral element in religion, led some among the Pharisees to think that he was their man, and that his evident genius could be harnessed to the task of restoring the religion of Israel as they thought that it ought to be. It is unlikely, however, that any of the Twelve had actually been Pharisees. Probably the majority of them belonged to that central group, educated in the solid piety of the synagogue, uncommitted to any particular party, but waiting for God in his own way to deliver his people.

What did they make of Jesus, when they encountered him and were called by him to his service?

All the records that we have stress the fact that they found him extremely difficult to understand, and that again and again they were perplexed by what he did and by what he said. This should not surprise us. People have always tried to fit Jesus into one familiar category or another; he always manages to elude them all, as life itself does. Jesus always breaks through the attempts of men to tie him down to this interpretation or that.

It is in Mark's Gospel that special stress is laid on this incomprehension in the minds of the disciples.

> Do you not yet perceive nor understand?
>   Are your hearts hardened?
> Having eyes, do you not see,
>   and having ears, do you not hear?
>   and do you not remember? . . .
> How is it that you do not understand?

(Mark 8: 17–21)

This Gospel was probably written for that Church in Rome to which Paul had written his greatest Epistle. Some have suggested that this writer specially stresses the stupidity of the disciples of Palestinian origin, as a reminder that, if a comparison had to be made, the inspired wisdom of Paul might seem more reliable as the foundation for a Church than the limited understanding of which these earlier apostles had shown themselves capable. This is possible. It is also possible that if, as tradition has always held, the recollections of Peter lie behind this Gospel, he was able better than any of the other writers to capture the actual historical situation, and to light up for us the perplexity through which he himself with the others had had gradually to find his way.

Jesus really was a revolutionary. He built on the Old Testament, but he always went beyond it. This meant that there were very few Old Testament terms that he could use to make clear the meaning of his own work. Should he claim to be the Messiah, the Anointed One, whom the Lord would send to do his work? As we have seen, there was no single accepted understanding of the term Messiah among the Jews. But politics played a great part in the interpretation of the term as held by all, or almost all, of those who held it at all. The first and all-important thing was to get rid of the Romans; after that the kingdom of God would come in due course. We have seen exactly the same phenomenon in our own time. President Kwame Nkrumah of Ghana expressed it quite frankly: "Seek ye first the political kingdom, and all these things shall be added to you". It is clear that, if Jesus had used of himself the term "Messiah", his hearers and his followers would have put him firmly into the political category.

Even though he did not use the term, all the records suggest the way in which all the time the disciples were adapting his teaching to the preconceptions which they already held. Jesus was the kind of man to make an overpowering impression on his contemporaries. He said that new times were coming in, that he himself was the beginning of the new time, in which God would be approachable as never before, and that God's power would be released as never before for the help and healing of his people.

In the Gospels hint after hint is given that the disciples could not get out of their minds the idea that Jesus had come to set up an earthly kingdom, in which they as his faithful followers would have positions of great prominence. Hence the strange request of the sons of Zebedee that they might sit on his right hand and on his left in his kingdom (Mark 10: 35-45). Even at the very end, the disciples were still disputing with one another as to who was to be the greatest in the kingdom (Luke 22: 24-27).

What, then, was it that distinguished these followers of Jesus from the rest? It was that with all their weaknesses they were still devoted to him. He had seemed to do all the wrong things. When the people were ready to take him by force and make him a king, he escaped out of their hands, and the golden opportunity was missed. And yet they were not prepared to forsake him, as so many had done (John 6: 66), and to go away. This is the significance of what is commonly known as Peter's confession. One thing that stands out in all the records of Jesus is that he was much more inclined to ask questions than to give answers. So he does not say "I am the Messiah". He asks them, "What do you think of me?" It is Peter who takes up the challenge and answers, "You are the Anointed One". In spite of all disappointments and frustrations, they are still sure that he is more than a teacher, more than a prophet. There could be many teachers and many prophets; there can only be one Jesus of Nazareth.

They had wanted to accept Jesus on their own terms and not on his, to think that they could tell him how Messiah should behave; gradually they must come to understand that they can accept him only on his own terms, and that, wherever he leads them, it will not be by the paths or to the goals that they had expected. This they would fully grasp only after the resurrection. For the moment faith in Jesus as Jesus was enough. The community of the faithful had come into existence.

One of the reasons for accepting as reliable the picture of the disciples presented to us in the Gospels is that it is so entirely free from idealization, and is in fact unflattering rather than the reverse. It is psychologically apt, as an account of the attempt of a group of average men to understand a leader whose gifts were so transcendently greater than their own.

CHAPTER THREE

UNWRITTEN TRADITIONS

The followers of Jesus became convinced that the resurrection had taken place. They had seen the risen Christ, and had talked with him. In the light of this astonishing experience, a completely new dimension had to be added to their thinking; every single idea they had ever had must now be thought out anew and from the ground up.

This was by no means a simple business. We have moved now from the world of Jesus' ministry to that of the Church after Pentecost. These early Christians did not all belong to the same language groups and cultural traditions. Like the original Palestinian disciples, they all brought to the business their own manner of thinking and different ways of trying to express what they had understood. We have to deal with no less than six distinct groups.

1. There were, first, the Jews who had always lived in Palestine, and who spoke only Aramaic, with at best a little colloquial Greek for business or official purposes. Language is a great divider. Palestine Jews, especially in Jerusalem, were on the whole conservative, suspicious of the Gentiles, concerned to maintain as far as possible the traditions of the Fathers, and not altogether friendly even to fellow Jews who spoke the Greek language.

The Dead Sea Scrolls have shown us that this Palestinian Judaism was not so hermetically sealed against outside influences as we had once thought. We find that at Qumran a number of "Hellenistic" expressions and ideas had already made themselves at home in the fortress of conservative Judaism. But this, in spite of such outside influences, was a Jewish world. Those among the Palestinian Jews who had become followers of Jesus Christ supposed that it would be possible to retain their Jewish identity in spite of their new-found belief that the Messiah had already come.

2. But not all Jews in Jerusalem spoke Aramaic. There was also a strong group of Greek-speaking Jews, permanently settled in Jerusalem, though they or their ancestors must at some time have returned from exile in Greek-speaking countries. The best-known representative of this group in the New Testament is the martyr Stephen. From his speech in Acts 7 it seems that Stephen may have belonged to that almost primitive sect among the Jews, which unlike the majority, believed that the building of the Temple had been a mistake— "God does not dwell in houses made by the hands of men" (Acts 7: 48–50). If this was the view of Stephen, he could quote the words put into the mouth of Jesus, "I will destroy this temple that is made with hands, and in three days I will build another, not made with hands" (Mark 14: 58. cf. John 2: 19). Paul, who developed further this view of the temple and the Law, may not have found himself without supporters even in Jewish circles in Jerusalem.

3. There were Jews permanently settled abroad, who had almost lost the use of the Aramaic language and both thought and spoke in Greek, but always retained their sense that Jerusalem was their true home. Pilgrimage played a great part in their lives. At every festival season Jerusalem would be crowded with pilgrims from every part of the Roman Empire. We know a good deal about one feast of Pentecost, because Luke has told us about it in Acts 2. We forget that Pentecost was celebrated thirty-seven times more before the outbreak of the Jewish war with Rome. Those who had believed on an earlier visit would come again to make contact with the mother

Church and to bring news of their brethren in the distant lands. Without moving from Jerusalem the apostles could carry on a great deal of missionary work. New believers would go home rejoicing, prepared to bring new churches into being in places which had not yet heard the good news.

4. Not all the visitors to Jerusalem were Jews by birth. Some had fully accepted the Jewish faith, and been admitted as proselytes. There was widespread interest in that faith; but many were held back from embracing it, because for a man to become a Jew meant accepting the necessity of circumcision, regarded by both Greeks and Romans as a barbarous and unseemly mutilation. The way was naturally easier for a woman. But the number of actual proselytes was never very large.

5. Larger, in all probability, was the number of those who had come under the influence of the Jewish Law, who attended the synagogue services and had abandoned every other form of religious faith, but had not committed themselves to acceptance of the whole Jewish law. It seems that the Christian Gospel made a special appeal to this class; they could retain all that was good and permanent in the Jewish law, and at the same time progress to the fuller salvation in Christ, without the necessity of submitting to circumcision. Why accept the sign when the fulfilment was already present?

6. Finally there were Gentiles who came directly to faith in Christ without any previous contact with the Jewish law or the Jewish way. To this group belonged such converts as the jailer in Philippi (Acts 16) and the few converts whom Paul won in Athens, the metropolis of Hellenic culture (Acts 17).

It would be a mistake to regard these groups as wholly separate one from another. In many cities of the empire several groups had to learn to live with one another, and did not find it at all easy to do so. This seems to have been the situation at Rome, when Paul wrote his letter to that Church a little more than twenty-five years after the death of Christ. There may have been a small nucleus of actual Jewish converts, but the letter itself does not suggest this. The other three groups—the proselytes, the "God-fearers" and the Gentile converts—were all certainly there, and found themselves involved in all kinds of disputes about keeping festivals and eating or not eating this and that. Paul wrote his letter to help them with the problem of peaceful co-existence in the one body of Christ.

There was not only this contact, and occasionally conflict, on the local scene. Apart from pilgrimage, already mentioned, the Roman empire was to an astonishing extent a scene of constant travel. Paul seems never to have experienced any difficulty in getting a ship to take him wherever he wanted to go. Evidence, both from the New Testament and from later Christian books, shows that the Churches could expect constantly to receive Christian visitors from other places. When they met they naturally talked with one another of what they knew of Christ, and shared their experiences.

What, then, was common to all these groups? What was it that made them Christians, and nothing else? We have already noted that this was the time of unwritten traditions. Christians talked a great deal and wrote down very little. If they did write anything down, nothing of it has directly survived. We can only infer what happened in this period by studying what was left at the end of it, and reconstructing as well as we can the strata which now lie buried under the surface of the New Testament.

On four points all Christians seem to have been agreed:

1. God has spoken and acted in Jesus Christ in such a way as to bring to an end the period of alienation due to human sin. The sign of the finality in God's act is the resurrection of Jesus Christ, through which the new creation is already here. Some Christians of that age seem to have doubted the reality of the resurrection, and the continuing fellowship with Jesus of Nazareth which it has made possible; Paul (1 Cor. 15) regards

such as having failed completely to understand the meaning of the apostolic preaching.

2. God has made Jesus of Nazareth "Lord and Christ". In this sense everything has been done, and there is nothing further that needs to be done. But the sovereignty of Jesus Christ, now hidden, needs to be declared and universally made manifest. For this purpose Jesus will come again in glory, probably very soon. That will be the final end and consummation of all earthly things.

3. The infant Church had as yet no scriptures of its own; but it had the Old Testament, which it now read through Christian eyes. Every Church believed that the Old Testament was full of foreshadowings of Christ; by looking back to the past, the Christian could understand what Christ came to do, and what he now is. A great deal of the time of the churches was spent on this task of Old Testament interpretation. There was not a single church in Christendom which was not profoundly affected by this study of the Old Testament.

4. Two practices distinguished the Christians from others. First, it seems from the start to have been taken for granted that all who believed in Jesus Christ, both men and women (Acts 8:12), would be baptized. And all who had been baptized would be partakers as often as possible in the common thanksgiving meal. It seems that both these rites were "eschatological" —looking to the time of the end. In baptism the believer became a part of the community which by faith already belonged to the new age. The meal called the Lord's Supper was an anticipation of the heavenly banquet, which God is preparing for all people, and in which the believers will be united for ever with their Lord. In later times both rites came to be closely associated with the death of Christ—baptism is dying with Christ and rising again (Rom. 6); the Lord's Supper is re-living with him (that is the meaning of the Hebrew word "remembrance") the events of the upper room and Calvary. But in the first period

the resurrection so dominated everything that the death of Christ seems to have been less central than it afterwards became.

As long as Christians expected that Jesus would come again very soon, they had no reason to be specially interested in the events of his earthly life. They were so fully occupied with the future that the immediate past was out of focus. The Jerusalem Christians were well acquainted with all the to-do that had been occasioned by the events concerning Jesus of Nazareth; they did not need to be specially reminded of them. But a change began to be observed as soon as the Gospel began to move out of the narrow world of Jerusalem and to touch men of other traditions and experiences. When the Gospel of new life in Jesus of Nazareth was presented to Gentiles, their natural question was, "And who was Jesus of Nazareth?" They did not know, and they needed to be told. This is reflected in an interesting manner in the first speech to Gentiles recorded by Luke in the Acts; when Peter speaks to Cornelius and his friends, he begins with an account of the ministry of Jesus, who went about doing good, a point not referred to in the earlier speeches delivered exclusively to Jews (Acts 10: 37–38). As time went on, questions repeatedly asked naturally received the same replies. A pattern of Christian answers to questions began to be formed.

Without doubt the part of the life of Christ about which connected answers first began to be given was the story of the Passion. This is the only part of his life about which we have anything like detailed information. In Mark's Gospel the story of the events of the last week of the Lord's life fills about one-third of the book. The same is true in only slightly smaller measure of the other three. This, together with the narratives of the resurrection, was what it was felt that every Christian ought to know. Probably within a few years of the death of

Christ the Passion narrative was beginning to take the shape which is familiar to us from our written Gospels.

This, however, was not the whole story. Any group which wishes to live the Christian life is certain to be faced with innumerable problems. Paul lights up for us in 1 Corinthians a problem by which his friends, trying to live as Christians in a particularly wicked Gentile city, were bound to be faced: Can a Christian partake of food which he knows to have been first offered to the pagan deities? (1 Cor. 8). This is still a burning problem for Christian converts in India. What in the world is the Christian to do? If he eats, he may seem to be rendering some kind of homage to those deities which he has repudiated. If he refuses to eat, is he not ascribing some kind of power to idols which he has now come to regard as nothing in the world?

When Christian groups were faced with such problems, the first question to be asked would naturally be, "Did Jesus himself say anything on this subject?" Those present would turn to the older members of the group who had actually heard Jesus preach, or who had been in contact with eye-witnesses and hearers of this word. On this particular question, as to what you may eat or drink, these witnesses did preserve a very interesting statement of Jesus, to the effect that what enters into a man from outside cannot defile him; Mark, by adding the comment "thus he declared all foods clean" (7: 19) makes it clear that in some circles at least this saying was understood in the sense, "It cannot do you any harm if you eat meat that has been sacrificed to an idol, since food is the gift of God." This did not answer all questions; so Paul finds it necessary (1 Cor. 10: 28–29) to add the very practical and commonsense argument that you should not think only of yourself but also of what your example may do to other people; the strong must be careful not to cause the weak to stumble.

This is a good example of the way in which sayings of Jesus

came to be preserved, and of the kind of discussions out of which the recollection of words and events was stimulated. It was in a living and growing community that the traditions about Jesus were developed and preserved.

But this development was more than just a recalling of the memories of old times. The minds of the believers were dominated by the resurrection. Whenever the believers gathered together there was a strong sense that the living Lord himself was in the midst of them. There was also a vivid realization of the power of the Spirit speaking through the inspired prophets and teachers through whom the life of the body was strengthened and edified. This has led some to think that the early Church did not make any clear distinction between words which the Lord had spoken in the days of his earthly life and those which were spoken in his name by his accredited messengers. Both, it is held, were attributed to Christ himself, and accorded equal authority. If this were so, it would mean that the Church itself in part created new traditions about Christ and did not merely preserve the old. But in point of fact there is no reason to think that this was so. Paul distinguishes quite clearly between those subjects on which he has a "word of the Lord" (he stresses a number of times the tradition which came to him from those who had been in Christ earlier than he (1 Cor. 15: 3)), and those on which he had no such word, and where he has to give his own judgement as one who has received the Spirit of Christ (1 Cor. 7: 25). What later came to be called the doctrine of the Ascension, though it is only rarely referred to directly in the New Testament, was clearly understood; there would be no further manifestations of the living Christ. He might still speak in visions, or through prophets; but then his words, as in the letters to the Churches in Revelation 2 and 3, would clearly refer to present situations, and not to conditions in Galilee and Judaea which had passed away. The Church was never in danger of confusing the present with the past; it saw its task as recalling and not as inventing.

This does not mean that all traditions were always repeated in exactly the same form and in the same words. In the first place, as the Gentile Churches grew, the traditions had more and more to be transmitted in Greek and not in Aramaic. The witnesses were more concerned with the sense than with the words. What is clearly the same tradition may come down to us in variant forms, as can be quite clearly seen by anyone who takes the trouble to compare the various forms in which our Lord's words at the institution of the Lord's Supper are recorded. The same incident or saying may be recorded in different contexts or with different applications; the parable of the good shepherd, as told by Matthew and Luke, does not illustrate exactly the same point in the two records. All that this amounts to is that the witnesses were human beings; they were not scholars compiling a systematic manual of doctrine, but practical people, trying to find their way, and to guide others, through the perplexing situations by which they were confronted.

Many of the stories about Jesus must have been told again and again in different congregations. As always happens to stories subject to endless repetition, these too would tend to settle down in fixed forms, and in many cases may have been familiar in these forms long before the evangelists incorporated them into their Gospels. Careful scholars think that they can identify seven main forms in which the traditions took shape before the period of Gospel-writing began.

1. An incident, often including a question, is briefly related, and leads up to a *decisive word* of Jesus. Thus, a most typical example, the little episode of Jesus eating with publicans and sinners, and the question of the scribes and Pharisees, leads up to the remark, "Those who are well have no need of a physician but those who are sick" (Mark 2: 17). The story is told not because it is in itself historically interesting, but because of the

picturesque and pregnant phrase to which it leads up.

2. *Stories of healing*. These are recorded not just as wonders, but as evidences of the presence in Jesus of the power of the kingdom of God. Here, too, the incident often closes with a saying of Jesus in which the significance of the episode is made plain; thus, when the servant of a Gentile centurion is healed, Jesus remarks, "Not even in Israel have I found such faith" (Matt. 8: 10).

3. *Parables*. These fall into two categories. Some are extremely brief—the kingdom of heaven is like—a man seeking goodly pearls, a treasure buried in a field (Matt. 13: 44–46). Some are extended stories, drawn from situations in everyday life, in which the teaching is in the story and must be worked out by each hearer for himself; the best known of these is the story which has come to be known as the Parable of the Prodigal Son (Luke 15: 11–32).

4. Little *collections of sayings* which seem to have no connection with one another, except that each contains one prominent word. These seem to have been brought together just in order to aid the memory. (A good example is the series of three brief sayings about salt brought together in Mark 9: 49–50.)

5. *Stories* told at considerable length. Scholars can point to parallels in style with other traditions of story-telling in both the Jewish and the Gentile worlds. In these there is much greater interest in the story itself than in the brief narratives to which we have already referred. Good examples are the healing of the demoniac in Mark 5: 1–20, and the curing of the epileptic boy in Mark 9: 14–29). In each of these there is high dramatic interest as well as profound spiritual teaching.

6. *Poems*. Much of the teaching of Jesus is preserved in the form of perfect Semitic poetry in which, as in the Psalms, the principle is that of parallelism (sometimes taking the form of antithesis) between two successive lines:

> So if your eye is sound,
>> your whole body will be full of light;
> but if your eye is not sound,
>> your whole body will be full of darkness.

(Matt. 6:22–23)

The poetic form gives a special solemnity to the teaching. But at the same time it serves as an aid to the memory—every schoolboy knows that it is much easier to learn poetry by heart than prose.

7. Stories about Jesus in which *a dimension beyond that of ordinary human experience* is introduced. The most striking among these is the narrative of the transfiguration (Mark 9: 1–13, etc.). But perhaps we should add also the story of the temptation, where the dramatic form reveals the deep conflicts in the mind of Jesus himself.

In the period of which we are speaking, these recollections about Jesus were circulating in the Churches for the most part as isolated units. There were also a great many other stories in circulation which have not come down to us. One such story has been preserved almost by accident. It is the view of all careful students that John 8: 1–11 did not form part of the Fourth Gospel as originally written. The evidence of the Greek manuscripts, some of which omit the passage, others of which place it after Luke 21: 38, supports a view which is based also on difference in style from the style of the Fourth Gospel. For one story which has been thus preserved hundreds must have been lost.

The aim of those who built up the traditions was to preserve as accurately as they could the words and works of Jesus. But we cannot exclude the possibility that at times those who heard misunderstood what they had heard. In Matthew 17: 27 Jesus is recorded as telling Peter to go and catch a fish, "and when you open its mouth, you will find a *stater*" (shekel). Many readers take this literally—there was an actual coin in the fish's mouth. Other devout students of the Scriptures think that here one of our Lord's vivid and imaginative sayings has been prosaically understood and made to suggest a miracle. What our Lord meant was, "Do they want us to pay taxes? All right, you are a fisherman; just go and catch a fish, and that will provide you with enough to pay both my taxes and yours". The astonishing thing is that we so rarely have to suspect such misunderstanding. Many of these fragments bear upon them the stamp of their own authenticity. The messengers of the Pharisees reported to them, "Never man spake like this man" (John 7: 46). The words and deeds of Jesus were marked by a certain originality, which makes him unlike any other man. It is this Jesus who emerges from the traditions, and challenges us with something unlike anything that we meet elsewhere.

But the time had to come in which the unwritten traditions would become fixed in written form.

CHAPTER FOUR

THE AGE OF THE THEOLOGIANS

The early Christians were so busy proclaiming the good news everywhere that they had little time to think of writing; nor do they seem to have regarded this as very important, since, like the other Jews, they regarded the living voice as a more important source of information than the written word. Yet a society in which people have learned to read and write cannot get on entirely without correspondence. We write to one another every day; it is not surprising that a large part of the New Testament is made up of letters.

Twenty-one of these letters have survived, and together make up slightly more than one-third of the New Testament. It is clear that what we have is only a minute fragment of what must once have existed. Paul was an active missionary for at least twenty-five years. If we suppose him to have written only one private letter a month, that would make three hundred letters, of which one only, the Epistle to Philemon, has survived. The same must be true of the other writers, one or two of whose letters we possess. We have no idea how it came about that just these letters and no others were preserved. Some readers must have regarded them as having some special importance, and so saw to it that they were not allowed to disappear as so much else has disappeared.

In no case can we say exactly when a New Testament letter was written, though for some we can fix the date within a year or two. Nor do we possess the other side of the correspondence, except in so far as Paul on occasion seems to be quoting letters that he has received. But in almost every case we can see that the letter is a real letter; it was written for good and urgent reasons, to meet some crisis, some situation that had arisen. Paul hears distressing rumours about his Galatian converts, and writes them a passionate tirade to call them back to that faith which they were in danger of abandoning. At another time a letter, apparently from the elders of the Corinthian Church, has told him of certain doubts by which they have been perplexed, and other sources have let him know of grave irregularities by which the life of that Church has been compromised. Hardly has he written his first letter to Corinth when a serious crisis arises, in which his authority over the Church which he has called into being is called in question, and he finds himself thrown on the defensive, and hastily writes a second, and perhaps a third, letter.

In letters written in this way, and some of them bearing the marks of considerable haste, the writers are not going to say all that they know. They will pull out of their minds and memories what seems relevant to the situation with which they are dealing, the arguments which are likely to convince the doubter or the adversary. If, therefore, we take each letter as it stands, we can see it as an example of the Christian mind at work on the continually changing material presented by a living and growing Church.

For our purpose in this study the special value of these letters lies in the fact that they fall roughly in the period between the time of the unwritten traditions and the period of Gospel-writing. Five of them almost certainly, and three others very probably, were written before the earliest of our Gospels saw the light. Two or three may be later than the latest of the Gospels. The rest probably fall within the Gospel-writing period. The earlier letters, then, judiciously used, can serve as a supplement and a correction to what we have inferred about the processes of thought that were going on in the earlier period.

The first Epistle to the Thessalonians was written almost certainly in the year A.D. 50; the career of Paul closed somewhere between A.D. 62 and 65. What do they show Christians to have been thinking about during those crucial years?

One of the first things that will strike any reader of the Epistles is that they have remarkably little to say directly about the earthly life of Jesus of Nazareth. How is this to be accounted for? One possibility is that the writers of these letters do not refer in detail to events in the life of Christ or to his words, because they could assume that all this was familiar to those to whom they were writing, and that there was no need to repeat that which was already known. We have seen reason to think that, especially among Gentile converts, there may have been considerable curiosity as to the life of the earthly Jesus. Some outline of his life may have been included in their preparation for baptism. The writer to the Hebrews, in 6: 1–2, gives a brief summary of what he understands the friends to whom he was writing to have learned as an elementary course of instruction in Christian faith and living—repentance, faith, baptism, resurrection, judgement. But he too urges his readers to go forward from this elementary stage to fuller knowledge—and this knowledge is to be directed not so much to what Christ was as to what he is, and to the privileges which Christians have in him.

Whatever the cause, the earthly life of Jesus is little dealt with in these letters. If we put together all the hints and references that are contained in them, we should still be far from being able to work out even an outline of his life and career, though we should learn a good deal about his death and resurrection. But what would confront us would be a variety of explanations of what the coming of Christ has meant for the whole human race, in particular for his Church, and therefore for us as individual human beings called into the fellowship of that Church.

A book which stands rather separate from the rest of the New Testament is the Epistle to the Hebrews, though here we may notice certain similarities with the doctrine set forth in the Fourth Gospel. Paul was certainly not the author, though there is much that is Pauline in the teaching of this writer. Perhaps he may have been Apollos, as Luther suggested; but we do not know. It is clear that this is a crisis epistle, directed to believers who were in danger of not going forward with Christ in a situation that demanded fuller dedication to him than they had as yet made. This is the supreme example in the New Testament of "prophecy" in the contemporary sense of that word—the illumination of the Person and Work of Christ by re-interpretation of Old Testament texts.

"What has Judaism that Christianity lacks?" asks the author. "Priesthood and a priest" would be the Jewish reply. "Not so", says the writer, "Jesus was certainly no priest after the old order, since he belonged to the non-priestly tribe of Judah. But look more closely. You will find in the Old Testament a clear promise of a new covenant; and you will find mysterious hints of a priesthood higher than that of the Aaronic line. Work it out in detail. Learn to think of Jesus as a priest, and you will find that you attain to a clearer understanding than ever before of who and what he is."

To develop his argument the writer does not need to dwell in detail on the earthly life of Jesus. Yet all the time he is coming back to him; it is clear that he is talking about an actual historical person, though he does not claim to have been an eyewitness of the events through which the Christian faith came into being. No writer in the New Testament has written more movingly of the real humanity of the one whom the Church had come to revere as the Son of God; he really became partaker of flesh and blood as men are, he knew as they do what it means to be tempted, and so is able to help them in time of need (2: 11-18). When the writer speaks of him as offering up "prayers and supplications with loud cries and tears to him who was able to save him from death" (5: 7), it seems clear that he is referring to the story of Gethsemane as we have it before us in the Gospels.

This is typical of all the theological writing in the New Testament. Inevitably theology is expressed largely in abstract terms; but behind the abstractions stands always the figure of a man, of a human being who really existed at a known and given time in human history, a known and given place on the earth's surface. The writer can assume that his readers will already know the outline of these facts to which his argument is related.

With Paul we come to one who stood nearer to the events of the life of Christ, and had had much to do with those who had been personal followers of the Lord, though he does not appear to have had contact himself with Jesus of Nazareth. (His claim, "Have I not seen Jesus our Lord?" (1 Cor. 9: 1), seems to refer to his vision on the road to Damascus.)

Paul in his letters deals with a vast variety of subjects; large books have been written expounding his theology. It is, however, possible to pick out certain recurrent themes which have stamped on this theology its special character. The three great pillars of Pauline theology are resurrection, Spirit, and reconciliation.

1. In his great defence of the doctrine of the resurrection, Paul affirms that, "if Christ has not been raised, then our preaching is in vain, and your faith is in vain" (1 Cor. 15: 14). What had made him a Christian was the experience of meeting Jesus of Nazareth as a living person, one who could speak to him, and to whom he could speak. To be a Christian means to be "risen with Christ" (Col. 3: 1), and to be partakers in that life in which the victory over death has been already achieved.

2. To Paul the Spirit is the central fact in the life of the

Church. When his friends in Galatia seem to be in danger of turning back from the adventure of faith to the works of the law, this is the heart of his appeal to them. What was it that faith had brought them that the law could not give? Surely the presence of the Spirit. "Does he who supplies the Spirit to you, and works miracles among you, do so by the works of the law, or by hearing with faith?" (Gal. 3: 5).

3. There was one thing that the law aimed at ineffectually, but which the Spirit effectively achieved—righteousness, being right with God. "That the righteousness demanded by the law might be fulfilled in us, who walk not according to the flesh but according to the Spirit" (Rom. 8: 4). Much of what Paul has to say on this subject is expressed in terms of "justification by faith", being accepted by God as righteous, while we are still sinners. But often Paul uses the simpler words "forgiveness" and "reconciliation" to make plain our changed relationship to God. He does not hesitate to say that "we were enemies to God" (Rom. 5: 10); so his urgent plea with his hearers is that they will allow themselves to be reconciled to God (2 Cor. 5: 20), who has reconciled us to himself (5: 18).

Each of the three terms which we have used is abstract. But each of them has a very concrete reference.

Resurrection. We are to be raised up by God. But who was it who was first raised up, and by his resurrection made our resurrection possible? The clear answer is Jesus of Nazareth, who is linked to the past in that he was born in the lineage of David the King, who is called Christ the anointed one, because in him all the promises made by God to Israel have been fulfilled, who has been declared Son of God by the resurrection, and whom we address as Lord because we have believed in him (Rom. 1: 3–4). *Spirit* in Paul, as in other New Testament writers, is not some vague indefinable power; the word always refers to the presence of the living Jesus Christ as dynamic within the life of the Church which is now understood to be

41

his body. At times it seems to be difficult to distinguish between Christ and the Spirit. In two consecutive verses we read "If Christ is in you"; "If the Spirit of him who raised up Jesus from the dead dwells in you" (Rom. 8: 10–11). In fact, however, the distinction is clear. We are told to become *like* Jesus Christ, that Christ is to be formed in us (Gal. 4: 19); we are never told to become *like* the Spirit. Jesus is the final and unalterable goal, the Spirit is the operative and moving power. But the Spirit is always the Spirit of Jesus, and cannot be understood at all without reference to him. It is the Spirit who brings Jesus of Nazareth near to us, and completes what he began.

God is always a *forgiving* God. But what he has now achieved is far more than the forgiveness of a few individual sinners; he has reconciled the whole world to himself; but this has been accomplished only in Christ (2 Cor. 5: 19). But those two small words "in Christ" sum up all that Jesus was and did, and of course as a climax his perfect obedience in the offering up of himself to death, together with the final victory in the resurrection. The historical events and the realities of faith are never separated from one another.

In the writings of Paul we can see the beginning of the development of Christian creeds. In 1 Thessalonians, which may be the earliest book in the New Testament collection and was certainly written not much more than twenty years after the death of Christ, Paul sums up what it was that Christians in Thessalonica had come to believe: "You turned to God from idols to serve a living and true God, and to wait for his Son from heaven, whom he raised from the dead, Jesus, who delivered us from the wrath to come" (1 Thess. 1: 9–10). Here we see almost all the essentials of the Gospel that Paul preached. It is to be noted that the Lord is referred to simply by his personal name Jesus. Paul is not quite consistent in his use of names; but, when he uses the name Jesus in this way, it is clear in almost every case that he is deliberately looking back to the "days of his flesh", to the man Jesus, and particularly to the weakness in which he was manifest in those days. (Compare 2 Corinthians 4 and the repeated use there of the simple name "Jesus".) The "Son" for whose coming the Thessalonians are to look is no mysterious and unknown figure descending from heaven, but is identical with the man of whom they have been told.

Now part of Paul's originality lies in his skill in interpreting his message in terms which his Gentile hearers would be likely to understand. No doubt he was not the first to attempt this, but he is the first whose writings have come down to us. Moreover, his letters were written to Christians, all of whom were being continuously exposed to the Old Testament in its Greek version, and who were therefore increasingly familiar with the Jewish tradition in religion. So we shall not expect in Paul radical departures from the Gospel as it had been preached in Jerusalem. But it will certainly be worth while to look closely at his writings, and to recognize traces of that "adaptation" to the situation of his hearers which is always part of successful missionary preaching.

"Jesus is Lord"

We have quoted one short Christian creed. We must now look at the shortest, and perhaps the earliest of all. "No man can say 'Lord Jesus' but by the Holy Spirit" (1 Cor. 12: 3; and compare "if you confess with your lips that Jesus is Lord" (Rom. 10: 9)). The Greek word *Kyrios*, Lord, is an extraordinarily interesting word. It is used sometimes as no more than a form of polite greeting, "Sir". But it came to be widely used in the Roman Empire of the Emperor, who at the time at which the New Testament books were written was already in the eastern provinces of the empire worshipped as a god. And shortly before the New Testament period, and to a far greater extent after it, the term *Kyrios* came to be used of the gods of the Graeco-Roman world. Thus we have from the third century a remarkable letter dug up from the rubbish heaps of Egypt in which X invites Y to be present "at the table of our Lord Serapis". What would a Greek-speaking Christian be thinking of, when he confessed his faith in Jesus Christ in the formula *Kyrios Iesous*?

The mystery religions of the Roman Empire are a most interesting phenomenon. Most of them centre on the figure of a dying and rising god, clearly a personification of nature, which dies in winter and is reborn in spring. Each had elaborate rites of initiation, in which it is even possible, though not certain in that early period, that the initiate was spoken of as being "born again". Initiates joined in a sacred meal, in which it was believed that they were in a mysterious way made partakers of the life of the god himself. Set forth in this bald way, the parallels between the mystery religions and Christian doctrine seem to be remarkably close. What can we confidently state about the connection between them?

A view which was widely held earlier in this century was that the key to our understanding of these Gentile Churches must be found in their worship. These small groups of Christians, in the life of which the celebration of the Eucharist played a dominant part, and in which the presence of the risen Lord was most intensely felt, would naturally feel themselves closely akin to the similar worshipping groups of the mystery-initiates. From them, it was suggested, they would naturally take over the title *Kyrios*, and all its mysterious associations with the presence of the god in the midst. God has made Jesus Lord; as divine Lord he is present in the midst of the believers. Some would go even further, and maintain that the whole idea of Jesus as a dying and rising God is derived from these mystery associations. How far have these views stood the test of time?

It is certain that the New Testament uses words which were widely current in "mystery" circles. It is certain that the experience of worship played a large part in determining the way in which Christians thought about Jesus Christ. It is probable that those who spoke Greek were influenced by the ideas that were circulating in the atmosphere around them, just as we today are all more influenced than we know by Marxist terms and usages. Beyond this we shall be a little cautious.

In the surviving literature of the first three centuries there is not one single case in which the ideas of the dying and rising god are made use of in relation to a known historical figure. All these gods belong to mythology and not to history. If the Churches did apply these ideas to Jesus, so far from following common practice, they did something for which as far as we know there was no precedent whatsoever. It is to be noted that the confession is *Kyrios Iesous*, and not *Kyrios Christos*. When the Jewish name *Iesous* is used, it is impossible to get away from a human person who was known to have lived under Tiberius Caesar, and whose death and resurrection were events remembered from recent times.

Gentile Christians may have picked up *Kyrios* as a divine title from their non-Christian friends. But this was not the only place in which they had heard it used. In the Old Testament in Greek as we now have it (the Septuagint) the mysterious name of God, YHWH, is represented by this same word *Kyrios*. All the copies of the Septuagint that we possess seem to have been made by Christians. It is now thought by some scholars that it was these Christians who substituted the word *Kyrios* for the older YHWH; but it is possible that the Greek word was introduced by the original translators. If so, this was a decision of immense importance, which can be accounted for only in terms of the sense of missionary vocation of these translators; this God of the Old Testament was to be presented not as the tribal god of the Jews but as the lord of all the nations. In the main *Kyrios* refers in the Septuagint to the God whom we call the Father; but even here there are hints of a wider use which would prepare the way for the transference of this divine title to the "Lord in the midst".

We may not suppose that only a Gentile Church could use the term "Lord" of the risen Jesus. In 1 Corinthians 16: 22 we have one of the few precious fragments of the Aramaic used by the early Church: *Maranatha*. This can be translated either "Our Lord comes" or "Our Lord, come". The parallel expression in Revelation 22: 20, "Come, Lord Jesus", suggests that the second translation is more likely to be that which Paul had in mind. There is reason to think that this prayer was used at the Eucharist, which Paul tells us (1 Cor. 11: 23 ff.) is to be observed "until he comes".[1]

No doubt there were considerable differences between the Aramaic-speaking Church in Jerusalem and the Churches of the great Greek-speaking cities of Asia Minor and the western lands (until well on in the second century the Church in Rome spoke Greek). These considerations, however, may help to remind us of the coming and going that was continually taking place, and to warn us against supposing that the difference was greater than it actually was.

This picture of trends, tendencies and emphases may have seemed unduly complicated to the reader who has been accustomed to take the New Testament as it stands, and devoutly to recite the Apostles' Creed every Sunday. But the work we have done in this chapter will not be without its use, if it helps to realize that what comes to us so easily comes only because men and women of old engaged in an immense labour of thought—trying to understand the Jesus whom they had known on earth or now knew by faith, trying to express their understanding in the most appropriate terms and to pass it on to coming generations. Jesus was far too great to be captured

[1] It does not, of course, follow that the Aramaic word would mean to those who used it exactly the same as the Greek word *Kyrios* with its other associations in the Greek-speaking world.

by any one formulation. Every possible expression had to be tried. Some, such as "servant", quite often used in the early days (Acts 4: 24, etc.) were found inadequate and were abandoned. Others proved their worth, and remained part of the Church's vocabulary. The value of what they did is shown by the fact that, though men have been pondering the work of Christ now for sixty generations, in all that time the Church has hardly added one single title to the many which are found in the New Testament itself.

CHAPTER FIVE

WHY DID PEOPLE EVER WRITE GOSPELS?

The early Christians seem to have written very little. It is likely that notes and flysheets circulated among them, making available to many those stories and sayings which originally depended on the memory of the few. It is probable that a connected narrative of the passion of Jesus was in existence not more than twenty-five years after his death. It is possible, though not certain, that those parts of the teaching of Jesus which are common to Matthew and Luke are drawn from an earlier work now lost and generally called by scholars "Q". But the first complete Gospel ever written may well be one which we possess, the Gospel according to Mark.

Why in the world did people ever begin to write Gospels? We cannot give an absolutely certain answer to that question; but we can list a number of considerations which may have led them to think that the time had come at which it would be well that the memory of Jesus should be preserved in written form.

The return of Jesus had been delayed much longer than the earliest Christians had expected. The generation of eyewitnesses was beginning to die out. As persecution became more severe, it seemed likely that the ranks of the survivors would rapidly be thinned. A time must be expected in which the living voice of the eyewitnesses would for ever be stilled (John 21: 21–23).

The capture and destruction of Jerusalem by the Romans in A.D. 70 was a shattering blow to the Christian Church no less than to the Jewish people. Up to that time there had always been a Mother Church. With this Paul himself had always felt it necessary to maintain the closest relations; he had taught his Gentile converts that they were bound to repay that Church for the spiritual benefits they had received from it by caring materially for its poor members (Rom. 15: 27). This was the fount of tradition, and also the divinely appointed censor, charged with the duty of seeing to it that the tradition was maintained intact. The Christians resembled the Jews in preferring the oral tradition to the written word. Now that there was no central control, they, like the Jews, came to think that the traditions must be written down to ensure their integrity.

The number of Christians was increasing rapidly, largely through the work of unknown and anonymous witnesses. While he lived, Paul had maintained "the care of all the Churches" (2 Cor. 11: 28), directly and through the young emissaries whom he used in his service. Even under his care grave errors had arisen in the Churches which he had founded and for the spiritual welfare of which he felt himself responsible. Now there was no one of equal authority to carry on the work. There would still be for a considerable time wandering emissaries; but these "prophets" had no recognizable commission (3 John 6–7), no authority other than that which they could establish by the quality of their preaching, and not all of them appear to have been highly reputable people. It was an urgent matter to make sure that the witnesses to the Gospel should know more exactly what it was that they had to proclaim, and that their message should be safeguarded against the possibility of distortion or diminution. The best remedy would appear to be a written manual available for their use.

It is often maintained that the early Christians were not interested in history. Whether this is to be taken as true or not depends on the interpretation to be given to the term history. It is true, if we understand by history what would be more correctly called the writing of annals, the setting down of bare facts and dates such as we find in some sections of the Book of Judges. It is true, if we think in terms of such history as is written in modern times, with constant reference to sources, and with all the apparatus of footnotes and appendices. It is not true in any other sense. The writers of the Gospels are intensely concerned about a person who for thirty-five years or so walked the stage of human history, whose career they believed to mark the climax, perhaps even the end, of human history, and whose memory they wished to preserve for all time among men. Fact, interpretation, communication—all these are indispensable ingredients in the writing of any history worthy of the name.

Again, it is sometimes said that the evangelists were not specially interested in biography. Judgement on this saying again depends on interpretation of the term. Certainly they were not concerned to write a life of Jesus which would contain everything that they knew about him. Most lives of this kind are unreadable. The evangelists could not include the letters of Jesus, because as far as we know he wrote none. Two of them did include genealogies, and thereby provided a nice crop of problems for interpreters. Between them they do not supply data by which we can determine with certainty either the date of the birth of Jesus or the year of his death. But, if biography is understood not as photography but as portraiture, the evangelists are unquestionably biographers. They set out to give a living portrait of a man. How far they have succeeded in their aim can be judged only by a reader who is prepared to take the trouble to read each of these little books straight through at a single sitting.

A Gospel is not quite like any other form of literature. Its centre is a person, but its primary concern is faith in that person. In one, the fourth, this aim is made quite explicit: "These things are written in order that you may believe that

Jesus is the Christ, the Son of God" (John 20: 31). In a second, the aim is described as being to give certain assurance to one who has already received some instruction in the Christian faith; this aim is to be achieved not by expounding a system of theology but by narrating a life (Luke 1: 1–4). In the other two Gospels this aim is less expressly stated. But in every Gospel the starting-point is faith in Jesus Christ, and the aim is the communication of that faith. This determines the selection and arrangement of the materials, what is included and what is omitted, and the character of the portrait that results.

How the writer set to work

In the first place it is important to remember that the size of the portrait was fixed for him by the canvas. Traditionally, a work which was intended to be readily accessible and easily read must be limited to what could be written on one papyrus roll, the material on which most books were produced at that time. Luke's Gospel is near to the limit of what could be so written, if the writing was not to become uncomfortably crowded on the roll. This means that selection must be careful, and that a great deal which might in itself be interesting must be omitted.

All the writers had lived within the Christian Church. They had been part of that tremendous process of telling and hearing, of listening and repeating, of coming and going, of which we have tried to give a description. We cannot be sure that the actual authors of our Gospels as we now have them had been themselves eyewitnesses of the events that they record; almost certainly they must have known apostles or their disciples, and have had opportunity to question them. They may have had access to some written records. It may be taken as certain that they knew a great deal more than they were able to record in the limited space at their disposal.

These writers were either Jews by birth or Christians who

had long been in contact with the Jewish traditions of the Old Testament. This means that they accepted without question the Jewish idea of a purpose of God in history, a purpose of which they saw the consummation in Jesus Christ. They were steeped in the Jewish idea of history-writing, in which history is seen as the meeting place of God and men. They were familiar with the great Old Testament biographies of Abraham, Moses and David. They wrote in the language of their time, and in an idiom that is largely unfamiliar and perhaps uncongenial to us in our more scientific age. They accepted without hesitation stories of the supernatural, believing that God is the sovereign ruler of the world and that Jesus was the instrument of his purpose, where we might be inclined to ask whether things happened exactly as they are described. This means that, if we wish to understand a Gospel, we must be prepared to make a certain effort of the imagination.

A Gospel is not at all like a book produced in the modern world. It does not carry within it the name of the author, or the date at which it was written or the place at which it was produced. Certain clues in early Christian books outside the New Testament provide us with some hints as to the identity of the authors. We are left to prudent inference for the discovery of place and date, and here certainty is beyond our reach. It is important not to exaggerate the length of time that elapsed between the ministry of Jesus and the date of the writing of the Gospels. It is almost certain that not more than forty years had passed before the writing of the earliest of our Gospels; probable that the four were complete within at most seventy years. Older men can recall with great precision striking events that happened forty years ago; and, as we have seen, the evangelists were not dependent simply on their own memories or on those of a small number of their friends. They were heirs of a great body of traditions on which they could draw.

Fifty years ago a distinguished scholar wrote that the Gospels must be seen as belonging to the level of popular or non-classical literature, and that the evangelists were compilers rather than authors. Unfortunately these phrases caught on, and for a whole generation hindered students from looking at the Gospels as they really are. It is, of course, true that the evangelists wrote in ordinary Greek as it was spoken in their time, with a good many signs of Old Testament influence; though Luke writes extraordinarily well, in point of style they cannot be compared with the great masters of Attic Greek. But each one of them is also a writer of genius; faced with the extremely difficult task of setting forth a tremendous theme in a book which can be read in an hour, each accomplished this task supremely well. These four little books have exercised a far greater influence on the history of the human race than any other literary compositions whatsoever.

Moreover, each of the evangelists was an outstanding theologian in his own right. Much of the work of scholarship in recent years had been occupied with tracking down sources or antecedent documents, and with analysing trends and traditions, and the modifications that traditions may have undergone in the course of the years and in different circles. This has led to a fragmentation of vision. In the last few years scholars have come to recognize that, when we have completed all this analysis as far as we are able, we still have to reckon with the finished product, to ask what exactly each evangelist was setting himself to do, what understanding of Jesus, in a word what theology, he was trying to express.

What is in the Gospels?

It is almost certain that Mark is the earliest of our four Gospels. The writer may have had before him a written narrative of the passion. Otherwise there is no reason to suppose that he had written sources. This gives him great freedom in the handling and arrangement of his material. What has he done with it?

53

The first thing that strikes a reader of the Gospel is that this is an intensely dramatic piece of work. Since the readers are Christians, they know what the end is going to be. But, by an astonishing effort of historical imagination, the writer has projected himself back into the time before the resurrection, and introduces us directly to the fears, the speculations, the uncertainties of that time. Over the second half of the Gospel rests a dark, brooding sense of destiny. From the moment of the arrival of Jesus in Jerusalem, the tension mounts, and is reflected in the strain which it is clear that Jesus himself is undergoing. Though the resurrection has twice been mentioned, no light from that hope falls on the mind of the disciples. Only one word of Jesus from the Cross is recorded, and that is the cry of apparent despair, "My God, my God, why hast thou forsaken me?" (15: 34).

It is possible that the writer has produced this dramatic effect simply from his own inner powers as a writer. But another and simpler explanation is possible. Very ancient tradition tells us that Mark is writing down what he had learned from the reminiscences of Peter. If this is really so, we can well understand how Peter, as he told the tales, would recall how it looked at the time to those who lived through those days.

Mark reveals to us plainly the questioning and perplexity caused by the appearance of Jesus. A second dramatic aspect of the Gospel is the series of attempts made by different people to answer the question, "Who is Jesus?" His enemies affirmed that his power was due to demonic possession (3: 22). The people were saying that he was a prophet, or perhaps *the* expected prophet (8: 27–28). His family thought that he was out of his mind (3: 21). A Gentile woman addresses him as "Lord" (7: 28; this may be no more than a title of courtesy, "Sir"). A blind man calls him by the clearly Messianic title "Son of David" (10: 48). Peter confesses faith in him as Messiah, but cannot take the further step and accept the idea of a suffering

Messiah (9: 29–33). Which of these is right? The correct answer is given, surprisingly, by another Gentile, the centurion standing at the Cross, "Truly this man was Son of God" (15: 39).

The way in which a writer plans his book is largely determined by the readers for whom his work is intended. We can see that Mark is writing for Gentiles, probably Gentile Christians, for whom he must carefully explain Jewish customs (7: 3–4). We can only infer his purpose in writing; but the guess may be hazarded that this little book was intended as a manual for preachers. This is the minimum that they must pass on, if non-Christians who have become interested are to know who it is in whom they are called to believe, and are to be led on step by step to a faith that cannot be shaken. The writer warns these preachers in advance of the questions they are likely to be asked by both Jews and Gentiles, and suggests the answers that can be found in a tradition going back to Jesus of Nazareth himself.

The contrast between Mark and Luke is obvious. Luke's is a sunlit Gospel. It opens with the narratives of the birth of Jesus—wholly Jewish in character, and perhaps the very earliest part of the Gospel story to be written down—which reflect the spontaneous joy of "the quiet in the land" at the realization that their hopes have been fulfilled. Luke does not overlook the opposition by which Jesus of Nazareth was dogged. Nor does he minimize the suffering of Jesus; he records more fully than the other evangelists the agony in the garden of Gethsemane (22: 39–46) and he alone records the striking saying "This is your hour and the power of darkness" (22: 53). But it is typical of him that he does not record the word of despair spoken from the Cross, and that the three utterances that he does preserve for us are all messages of hope and consolation. Again and again he records the joy that came with the presence of Jesus: "all the people rejoiced at all the glorious things that were done by him" (13: 17).

55

This is a Gospel of human interest and human relationships. Mark represents Jesus, sometimes almost abruptly, in his deeds rather than in his words. Luke sees him in his relationships with all kinds of people and records many sayings that are not found in any other Gospel. The parables take on a more human form, and in a number of cases take the shape of quite lengthy stories drawn from human experience. If a Christian without expert knowledge were asked to name the two stories and the two incidents that had most deeply impressed him, he might well name the parables of the Good Samaritan (10: 25-37) and the Prodigal Son (15: 11-32), and the stories of the woman that was a sinner (7: 36-50) and of Zacchaeus (19: 1-10). This would be a good choice—almost the whole Gospel is contained in these four passages, and all the four are known to us from St. Luke's Gospel only.

One fresh problem confronts us here. There can be no doubt that Luke had Mark's Gospel before him and made extensive use of it. It is illuminating to see how one evangelist uses the work of another. Clearly Luke regards himself as entitled to great freedom in the use of this material. He does not hesitate to improve Mark's Greek, and even extensively to rewrite passages that he is clearly taking over from him. He does not feel himself tied to any chronological framework, and places incidents recorded by Mark where they will fit in with his own plan and not in the context in which they were originally found.

These methods result in important differences between the two Gospels. There is an even more fundamental change in atmosphere. The earliest Christians, as we have several times noted, believed that Jesus would come back very soon. Gradually it became plain to them that the interval would be longer than they had supposed, and that the work of Christian witness must be understood in larger dimensions than they had at first realized. Luke was perhaps the first great Christian theologian to understand to the full the significance of this change. He was himself a Gentile Christian; he was writing in the first place for an educated Gentile reader. One of his main concerns is the proclamation of the Gospel to the nations of the world, and he has some idea of the length of time that this may be expected to take. Old Testament writers had a clear understanding of history; Luke is the first Christian thinker to take up this Old Testament idea and to rethink it in the light of the revelation in Christ. His writings, as we might expect, are full of subtle allusions to the historical books of the Old Testament.

In Jesus God has spoken his final word to men. But history has not come to an end; it has simply entered on a new period. The Church is not simply the expectant body, waiting for the coming of Christ in triumph; it is the proclaiming Church, occupied with a task which will fill the entire interval between the resurrection and the final triumph, however long that may turn out to be. For that reason Luke, and he alone among the four evangelists, links the Gospel directly to secular history (3: 1-2) by naming the secular and spiritual rulers of the time. He sees the Church as an entity in history, which has a historical beginning, and lives on the stage of the history of the world within which it is a creative force. It is this that makes his Gospel specially valuable to us, who are well aware of history as one of the problems at our own door. We are still engaged in the task of making known the One who was given as an illumination for the Gentiles (2: 32); we know far better than Luke could ever have guessed the length of the period of the Church's history; at times we feel that we are still only at the beginning of the task.

With Matthew the atmosphere has changed once again. This is the only one of the four Gospels that appears to have been written for a Church, and possibly for reading aloud in the Church's worship. It is a very carefully constructed work. It is built up of five great blocks of material, each marked by a notable discourse of Jesus Christ (5-7, 10, etc.; discourses which we can see from comparison with Luke to have been brought together in their present form by Matthew himself). There is an introduction dealing with the birth of Jesus, and an appendix dealing with his resurrection. Matthew has almost certainly used Mark, and follows him rather closely in many sections; but, like Luke, treats Mark with the freedom of one who is himself an author and not merely a copyist (compare Matthew 9: 1–8 with Mark 2: 1–12, and Matthew 8: 28–34 with Mark 5: 1–20).

It is commonly said that Matthew is the most Jewish of the four Gospels. In one sense this is true. Matthew quotes the Old Testament frequently, and finds fulfilment of prophecy where we might be unlikely to find it. Jesus is presented as the King of the Jews; the sin of the Jews, for which the kingdom is taken away from them (21: 43), is their refusal to recognize and acknowledge their King. But the real purpose for which the Gospel is written is not always understood.

It is written for a Church which is in danger of losing its first love, and for this reason it is full of warnings. Matthew indicates what is to follow in the first story that he tells after the birth of Jesus. The story of the wise men (2: 1–12) is about some men who knew hardly anything and yet, using the little that they had, found the king of the Jews, and about other men who knew everything, even down to the detail as to where that king was to be born, and found nothing. Matthew is saying to his readers, "It happened to them; it could happen to you. The kingdom has been given to you, but it could be taken from you, as it was taken from the Jews". Hence the reiterated emphasis on judgement, on those who will be cast out into the place of weeping and gnashing of teeth, words which sometimes ring harshly in our ears. Only in this Gospel does the Son of man sit as king in judgement, and divide irrevocably the sheep from the goats (25: 31–46).

With the Gospel of John we are in a different world. Once again the evangelistic character of the message is stressed—these things are written that men might believe (20: 31). We do not know who the intended readers were nor where they lived. Some have thought that they were already believers, whose faith needed to be strengthened; others have thought of Greek-speaking Jews in one of the great cities of the Roman Empire, who had a deep knowledge of the Old Testament and were not unfamiliar with Greek philosophy, but had begun to be interested in the Christian Gospel. The aim of the writer would then be to show them that only in Christ would they find the synthesis of all the scattered lights of wisdom that had come to them in various ways.

At the beginning of this century many scholars regarded this Gospel as strongly "Hellenistic" in character, as the free composition of a profound Christian thinker who was more at home in the Greek than the Jewish world, and as therefore having very little historical value. More recent study has stressed the Jewish element in the work. Clearly the author knew a good deal about Jerusalem, perhaps at first hand. Thus, for instance, we know that there really was a pool in Jerusalem with five porticoes (5: 2)—the remains of it have been discovered—and this may well be the very pool at which the miracle of healing is recorded as having taken place. And the experts in Jewish Rabbinic theology tell us that much of the argument in this Gospel resembles closely the type of argument which is to be found in Jewish works written a little later than the Gospel.

The Gospel opens with a solemn hymn about the *logos*, the Word of God. Since this "logos-theology" is not found in any other part of the Gospel, and certain words such as "grace" (1: 14, 16, 17) do not recur, some have thought that the writer is here making use of an older hymn which was already current in the Church. This is quite possible, but only moves back one stage the question as to the source of this hymn and its remarkable theology. The word "logos" had a long history in Greek and was used in a variety of senses. It can mean "word", and also "reason", and also that principle of proportion by which the world is held together. In Jewish literature in Greek (Wisdom, Philo) the *logos* is one of the mediators between God and man, but is never fully divine nor fully personal. No doubt the writer was familiar with these usages—it is impossible to write in Greek without using Greek words, and every word carries with it its own history. But the view is gaining ground that in his prologue the writer is offering us an inspired commentary on Genesis 1. All the great archetypes of that great chapter are here—word, light, life, creation. It makes a magnificent introduction to what the writer has to tell us of the Word made flesh, the eternal Word which actually and completely assumed human nature in all its poverty and weakness. (That is what the word "flesh" seems to mean; it does not imply sinfulness, though it may carry also the idea of perishableness.)

The prologue also introduces us to a peculiarity of the author's method of writing which presents difficulties to those who are not familiar with it. He announces something, and then proceeds to meditate, to enlarge upon it until it is clear that what we are listening to is the voice of the evangelist, and not the voice of the Lord or of the original tradition. In chapter 3, he starts by giving us the striking story of the conversation of Jesus with Nicodemus about the new birth, or the birth from above. By the time that we have reached verses 18 to 22, the voice of Jesus is hardly heard at all—it is the evangelist who is commenting on the story that he has told, and which he believes to be an event of history. But where exactly does the transition take place? It is extraordinarily difficult to say; this helps to give its mysterious quality to a book the simplicity of which is all on the surface, but which, as we ponder it more deeply, shows that it has ever greater depths to disclose to us.

It is at once evident that there are great differences between the first three Gospels and the Fourth. The question whether the writer of this Gospel knew the other three is still debated, and different views are held; the most recent research tends to hold that the writer does not at any point show familiarity with the Synoptic Gospels as we have them. His work is based on an independent tradition, which at certain points happens to overlap the traditions especially of Mark and Luke. This by no means implies that his tradition is less valuable than that of the other three, though his method of handling his material is very different from theirs. He is no romancer, making up stories out of his own head; he is a responsible historian, presenting what he believes to be a valid picture of one through whom the destiny of the human race has been fulfilled.

It is his aim to show the descent of the eternal into time. To effect this, he writes in terms of certain pairs of words, in which sharp antitheses are expressed—light and darkness, spirit and flesh and so on; but these deal with moral contrasts and moral choice, which in the end is the choice between believing and unbelief, between obedience and rebellion. Yet he never forgets that he is writing the history of a man. Little human touches abound in the Gospel (as in 4: 6); these do not come in at random; they are deliberately placed there to remind us that it is a human life with which we are concerned and by our response to which we are inescapably judged.

This, no less than Mark, is a dramatic presentation. Chapters 2–4 present us with the challenge to believe. Chapters 5–12 show conflict between faith and unbelief, and faith gradually standing out more clearly as the shadows of unbelief deepen. In Chapters 13–17 we see the strengthening of faith in preparation for a fearful testing. In 18 and 19 we see the apparent triumph of unbelief; but in 20 and 21 faith is restored and vindicated by the real triumph of the resurrection. And the

61

Gospel ends with the challenge to the reader: On which side do you stand? You cannot have it both ways.

So we have the four presentations.

Mark offers us the Servant of the Lord, always active, known in his deeds and also in his words.

Luke shows us the approachable redeemer, the friend of sinners and the bringer of human joy.

Matthew depicts the King of the Jews, but warns us against rejecting the very one whom we profess to have accepted.

John shows the eternal Word of God present in flesh in the world, and by his presence assuring the victory of the light over the darkness.

How are we to use these four? Which of them shall we prefer? How shall we try to combine them? Or shall we not try to combine them, but let each stand on its merits, each as a pointer to a central mystery which is too great to be expressed by any one of them, or by all the four together?

This must be the subject of our final chapter. The aim of our study is practical—to answer the question: How do we read the Gospels today? But before we come to this, we must ask the most important question of all—What did Jesus himself think about it all? How near can we come to him, and to an understanding of his mind and purpose in his ministry, in life, in death and in resurrection?

CHAPTER SIX

WHAT JESUS THOUGHT ABOUT HIMSELF

The reader who has followed the argument so far may find himself led to agree that, though the New Testament should command our deepest reverence as the book in which the words of life are given, this should not prevent our making use of a critical approach, and honestly asking the questions that are presented to us by the records themselves. Our aim is to come as near to Jesus as we can. In part we do this by surrendering ourselves to the impact made upon us by each single Gospel as a whole. We do not dishonour them if we try to go behind them, and listen separately to the various voices of which their complex harmony is made up.

We have seen that fact and interpretation are closely blended on every page of the Gospels; but that at certain points it is possible to distinguish between the fact and the interpretation.

It is widely held today that the interpretation of the parable of the tares in Matthew 13: 37–43, though it is ascribed to Jesus himself, was actually worked out by the Church in the light of what it understood Jesus to mean, and as it tried to apply the words that he had spoken to its own problems and needs.

In Mark 14: 24 we read "This is my blood of the covenant, which is poured out for many"; but in Matthew 26: 28 "which is poured out for many for the forgiveness of sins". It is practically certain that the last five words are an interpretation added by Matthew—undoubtedly correct interpretation, but it is unlikely that these words were spoken by Jesus Christ himself.

If we wish to come as close to Jesus as possible, one method is to put on one side for the moment those passages in which interpretation seems to have played a considerable part, and to start from those parts of the Gospels in which the records seem to give as nearly as possible the words which Jesus himself spoke and in the form in which he spoke them. We certainly shall not perfectly succeed; we may find that the effort is in itself rewarding.

Let us consider some of the titles by which Jesus himself spoke of himself and his work, and consider how far this method will carry us towards understanding.

1. We noted that the people spoke of Jesus as "the prophet" or "one of the prophets". It seems that Jesus himself did not refuse to think of himself in this way. One of the most striking of his sayings is "I must go on my way today and tomorrow, and the day following; for it cannot be that a prophet should perish away from Jerusalem" (Luke 13: 33). It is clear that he here identifies his vocation as that of a prophet, and this not in the sense of one who proclaims the future, but of one who proclaims the word of the Lord, and will meet with death at the hands of his fellow-countrymen as a reward for his pains.

But there is something in Jesus that goes beyond what had ever been claimed by any other prophet. The healings carried out by Jesus are evident signs that God is at work in a new way to restore man to what it had always been the intention of God that he should be. But there is a new emphasis—not simply on God and his work, but on the one through whom that work is done. What do men think of Jesus? Do they accept him or reject him? Whatever Jesus is saying or doing, this question is never far away.

The claim of Jesus to be both a prophet and more than a prophet is made clear in his attitude to John the Baptist. He speaks of John the Baptist in terms of the highest praise; among the sons of men there has been none greater than he. "All the prophets and the law prophesied until John" (Matt. 11: 13), a

64

very difficult saying, and one which just because of its difficulty is likely to have been preserved in the form in which Jesus spoke the words (cf. Luke 16: 16). They seem to mean that John marked the end of an epoch; prophets in the past had all been those who made ready the way of the Lord, but now the Lord himself is coming in an entirely new way, and, though Jesus for the moment identifies himself with the prophets, he stands in a relationship to the Lord different from that of any of those who had come before him.

What everyone noticed in Jesus was his authority. This comes out in all the records. Special interest, therefore, attaches to his answer to the question addressed to him by the chief priests and elders, "By what authority are you doing these things? or who gave you this authority to do them?" (Mark 11: 28). Following his usual practice, Jesus answers by asking another question—Was the baptism of John the Baptist from heaven (i.e., commanded by God himself) or from men (i.e., dependent upon some human authorization)? Jesus is not, of course, suggesting that his own authority was derived from his baptism by John. He is appealing to common sense and spiritual perception. A prophet has no credentials other than the intrinsic power of his message. But, if the ministry of John who did no miracles was "from heaven", more certainly is the ministry of Jesus clothed with the authority of "heaven"; so, if the Jews lacked discernment to recognize the authority of John, more certainly will they be unable to understand who Jesus is, and by what authority he does what he does.

More than in any other place the authority claimed by Jesus stands out in his revision of the ancient law: "You have heard that it was said by them of old time . . . but I say unto you" (Matt. 4: 21–22; 27–28; 33–34; 38–39). It is almost certain that Matthew has collected into one great "Sermon on the Mount" sayings uttered by Jesus on many different occasions, and that to some extent he has edited them; but we cannot possibly eliminate this startling claim of Jesus. All Jewish Christians were faced by the problem of the extent to which the law of Moses was still binding on them; we can see in Matthew's Gospel traces of the views of those Christians, known to us also from the Acts of the Apostles, who believed that Jesus had added to the Law the truth of his own Messiahship, but had not abrogated any part of it. All the more startling is it to find in this Gospel the calm "I say unto you . . ." by which the new law is introduced.

It is scarcely possible to exaggerate the veneration in which Moses was held by the Jewish people in the time of Christ. He was the great lawgiver. But, far more than that, he was the man with whom God had spoken face to face, as a man speaks with his friend (Num. 12: 7). He fulfilled in relation to the people the threefold function of prophet, priest and king. To speak against his authority was to speak against the authority of God. And here is a young man, who had never had an education, calmly standing up and affirming that he can, not abrogate the ancient law, but fill it with such new meaning that it becomes only a historical stage in man's awareness of the divine, and not the final word of God to man. It is not surprising that some were ready to accuse him of blasphemy.

2. This consideration leads straight on to the heart of Jesus' message—the Kingdom of God. This term is misleading in English. To use the word "kingdom" tends to suggest a geographical area, the United Kingdom, or the people who inhabit that area and all of whom accept the authority of one single sovereign. The term "the Kingdom of God" in both Hebrew and Greek, means "the Sovereignty of God"—not just his supreme rule as Creator over heaven and earth, but that relationship which comes into existence where, and only where, the Will of God is freely and joyfully accepted by men. It is clear that this kingdom may be invisible, or may be re-

cognized only through certain signs of its presence, or may be visible when God has everywhere overcome the rebellion in the hearts of men and rules over a loyal and grateful people.

In what sense did Jesus proclaim the kingdom? On this subject three views have been held. (a) The kingdom is "eschatological", to use a piece of jargon which has unfortunately become current in theological writing; it will come only at the end of all things, when God has subdued all things to himself. (b) The kingdom is "at hand"—it is not here yet, but it will come very soon. On this view, Jesus believed that his own death would introduce the crisis that would lead to the coming of the kingdom. (c) The kingdom is already here, because Jesus is here. Whatever truth there may be in the other two, a place must certainly be found for this third interpretation. In another of his remarkable and difficult sayings, Jesus tells his enemies that "if it is by the finger of God that I cast out demons, then the Kingdom of God has come upon you" (Luke 11: 20). We do not know what Aramaic word Jesus used. There can be no doubt whatever as to the meaning of the Greek word *ephthasen*; it cannot mean "will come upon you"; it can only mean "it has come upon you when you did not expect it; it has caught you anawares; it is here already and you have not noticed the fact". As elsewhere, the stress is on the first person. The fact that devils are being cast out does not in itself indicate the presence of the Kingdom of God—that could be a fake or magic or the work of evil spirits—but when *I* cast them out, take note of what is in your midst. "The Kingdom of God is within you" (Luke 17: 21 A.V.; "in the midst of you" R.S.V.) is not, as has so often been imagined, a reference to the mystical indwelling of God in the hearts of men; it is a statement, both menacing and consoling, that where Jesus is the Kingdom of God is visibly present.

Closely related to this controversy is the terrible warning proclaimed against those who refuse to see the work of God, when it is plainly set forth before their eyes. "Whoever blasphemes against the Holy Spirit never has forgiveness, but is guilty of an eternal sin" (Mark 3: 29). Mark makes plain the occasion of this terrifying judgement: "for they said, He has an unclean spirit". Jesus had been performing before them the signs of love; the best that they can do is to say that his works are the manifestation of diabolic power. If a man sees what is good and says that it is evil, if he has so totally lost his capacity to distinguish between good and evil, can even God give it back to him? God judges no man, and yet men are judged. Jesus Christ is the *crisis*, the occasion of discrimination among men; by what they think of him, by their reaction to him, men reveal what is in the depths of their hearts, and so they are judged.

Jesus was calling Israel from being the people of the law into being the people of the kingdom, which was visibly present in himself. When the people had finally rejected this summons, and the world became the world in which Jesus Christ had been crucified, the nature of the message had to be changed. In its proclamation the earliest Church spoke little about the kingdom; the idea was not forgotten (e.g., Rom. 14: 7), but it had as it were gone underground, its place being taken by the Church. The Church, the Body of Christ, is not the Kingdom of God, which now is the hope, the promise for the future; it is that body to which is committed the duty of setting up the signs of the kingdom, those evidences that the kingdom, though hidden, is still the great reality in the life of man.

3. The Church from the beginning has expressed its faith in "Jesus Christ our Lord". "Christ" has come to be to us little more than a proper name, just as is the word "Christian". But "Christ" is in reality very far from being a proper name; it means "the Lord's anointed", representing the Hebrew "Messiah". In using the term, the Church affirms unmistakably

68

that it judges itself to be the heir of all the Old Testament promises, since it has accepted as Lord the one to whom they all point.

How far back does this identification go? Can we say that Jesus regarded himself as the Messiah of the Jews? Here we can only return the ambiguous answer Yes and No. Yes, in the sense that he knew himself to be the one in whom all the promises of God would become Yea and Amen (2 Cor. 1: 20). And yet it was hardly possible for him to use of himself any of the current terms of Jewish expectation, since all were loaded with secondary meanings which he must reject. As we have seen, there was no one single form of Messianic expectation among the Jews. Yet, if there was one feature which was common to almost all of them it was the hope of the restoration of the earthly kingdom, a Son of David sitting on the throne of his fathers in Jerusalem and exercising an earthly sovereignty in the name of the Lord. We have seen the difficulty experienced by Jesus in setting free even his own intimate disciples from a Messianic idea to which they obstinately clung. It is easy to understand, therefore, why he never directly used the term "Messiah" of himself—to have done so would have been to strengthen the hold on the minds of his hearers of precisely those wrong ideas from which it was his purpose to set them free.

On the other hand, he does give to those who were prepared to think things through, indications which can only be called Messianic. When John the Baptist sent disciples to ask Jesus whether he was the one who was to come, or whether another is still to be expected (Matt. 11: 1–4), he described his own work in words which clearly recall Isaiah 61: 1–3; that passage refers to "the acceptable year of the Lord", and this can hardly be understood as other than the Messianic age.

When he asks the disciples who they think that he is, and Peter answers "Thou art the Christ" (Mark 8: 27 ff.), he does not reject the title but tells them that this is a secret which is not to be divulged to others. The importance of this incident, which is presented in all the Gospels as a turning-point in the ministry of Jesus, is not that Peter greets him as the Messiah, but that he does so in spite of the fact that Jesus had done none of the things that Messiah was expected to do, and had shown no signs of attempting to win for himself a political kingdom.

4. The most characteristic of all the titles by which Jesus refers to himself in the Gospels is "Son of man", a perplexing title as to the exact meaning of which whole libraries of large books have been written.

In the first place it is to be noted that no one else ever addresses Jesus by this title. A second major difficulty is that in certain sayings, as reported in the Gospels, Jesus himself seems to make a distinction between himself and the Son of man: "Whoever . . . is ashamed of me and of my words . . . of him will the Son of man also be ashamed, when he comes in the glory of his Father with the holy angels" (Mark 8: 38). This seems to be a curious way of putting it, if Jesus and the Son of man are the same person.

Thirdly, we simply do not know the origin of the term.

"Son of man" in Hebrew or Aramaic can mean simply "a man", and nothing more. In Ezekiel, the prophet in his experience of divine revelation is again and again addressed by the Lord as "Son of man" (e.g., 13: 1; 14: 3, etc.). Some have thought that Jesus took over this turn of phrase to indicate that he also was a man to whom in a special way divine revelation came.

In Daniel 7: 13 one like to a son of man is given dominion and glory and a kingdom. The earthly kingdoms symbolized by the beasts are done away; but the kingdom of this Son of man, who is explained to be "the saints of the most High", that is, the people of Israel, receives a kingdom which they shall possess for ever and ever (7:18). Without doubt this passage had great influence on the mind of Jesus himself and on the mind of the Church. But it is to be noted (and this is stressed by some excellent scholars) that this is the title not of an individual but of a faithful people; it is maintained by some that the term is always to be understood in a corporate sense—Jesus and his faithful people; never Jesus alone.

Then, as we noticed in Chapter Two, the Son of man is a conspicuous figure in the Book of Enoch, one who is reserved with God until the time of the end, and to whom judgement and victory are committed. The trouble is that we simply do not know whether Jesus or anyone else in the circles in which he moved had ever heard of the Book of Enoch or was familiar with the kind of language which it uses. And it is possible that the section of the Book of Enoch in which the Son of man passages occur, so far from having influenced the language of the New Testament, was itself written under New Testament influence.

Finally we have the problem that some of the Son of man sayings refer to a manifestation in glory ("They they will see the Son of man coming in a cloud with power and great glory", Luke 21: 27); whereas others seem to refer to a present time of weakness and rejection—"the Son of man has nowhere to lay his head" (Luke 9: 58).

The debate about these problems will go on for a very long time. From it we can draw out at the present time three points on which there would be general, but not universal, agreement.

(a). That Jesus did use this term of himself, and that no one else used it of him.

(b). That the term was mysterious, not readily understood by those who heard it, and that it was deliberately chosen for this reason, since it was always the purpose of Jesus to challenge and not to explain, to present himself to the eyes of faith and not to compel faith by a plain disclosure of who he was.

(c). That in his mind and in that of his hearers there would certainly be an association between this term and the idea of a kingdom, and that therefore there would always be an implied contrast between the present situation of one who certainly was not a king and the coming of the kingdom to which he certainly looked forward.

5. One of the regular Muslim objections to the use of the term "Son of God" by Christians is that Jesus himself never used it and was himself content to be no more than a prophet.

The Muslims are not quite correct in their statement of the case. In John 10: 36 Jesus replies to the Jews, "Do you say of him . . . You are blaspheming, because I said, I am the Son of God?"; and this clearly implies a claim to which the Jews were taking violent objection. But we shall not make use of that argument in this connection, since we have recognized that in the Fourth Gospel there is a larger element of interpretation than in the other three, and that we must be careful not to take as actual words of Jesus what may in fact be the inspired meditation of the writer.

Our study is to be concentrated more on the word "Father" than on the word "Son". And here we are not dependent on one quotation or one source; in every source and in every tradition we find Jesus speaking of "my Father in heaven", or addressing him directly as "Father". This is confirmed by a most interesting piece of evidence outside the Gospels. A very few words of Semitic origin survived in the traditions even of the Greek-speaking Churches; one of them was the word "Abba", Father, which the disciples had so often heard on the lips of Jesus himself. So Paul reminds the Roman Christians that, when they pray, perhaps in times of great distress, when a man hardly knows what he is saying (8: 26, 27), the word that spontaneously rises to his lips is "Abba" (8: 15), the very word which Jesus himself is recorded to have used in his time of greatest trial, in the garden of Gethsemane (Mark

72

14: 36), and twice to have repeated on the Cross (Luke 23: 34, 46).

We might be inclined to ask whether there is anything so very special in this. There is a widespread impression that the fatherhood of God and the brotherhood of man are abstract principles which are common to all religions, and that Jesus had simply made these his own and proclaimed them as central to his message. Nothing could be further from the truth.

Here we are dependent on the testimony of the experts. It is quite true that in the Old Testament God is sometimes spoken of as the Father of Israel (Isaiah 64: 8: "Yet, O Lord, thou art our Father . . ."). But those who have most carefully studied the evidence for Jewish practice at the time of Christ, tell us that it was not the custom for this particular term or form "Abba" to be used in addressing God. That Jesus did so use it left an indelible impression on the minds of the disciples precisely because this was something that they were not accustomed to hear.

This way of speaking with God seems to indicate an awareness of a relationship to God which is not exactly the same as that of other men. This is expressed most clearly in the great poetic outburst, "No one knows the Son except the Father, and no one knows the Father except the Son" (Matt. 11: 27), a passage which startles us by its likeness to the utterances of Jesus in the Fourth Gospel. But the thought is something that is diffused throughout the Gospels as a whole, and cannot be pinned down to one quotation or to one tradition.

Moreover, though this relationship between Jesus and the Father is unique, it is not exclusive; it is into a relationship to the Father similar to his own that he calls the disciples, in virtue of an act of total and final self-commitment to the cause of God of which he himself has given the model and the example. He teaches them to pray "Our Father" or "Father". Nothing could be more misleading than to think that this is a general form of address in which all men may indiscriminately join. It is a prayer of discipleship. Who is this Father? It is the Father of Jesus, who can be addressed as Father only because he has this particular Son. Who can address him as Father? Only those who by obedience to the Son Jesus Christ have obtained what Paul was later to call "the adoption", and so have the right to address him in the terms which they have learned from Jesus Christ.

6. This leads us on to the final point—the supreme self-confidence with which Jesus places himself in the centre of the stage. It has often been said that the message of Jesus was a message about God, and that only later the disciples turned it into a message about Jesus himself. This is only very partially true. He is convinced that, in meeting him, men are encountering the final and decisive challenge, and that by their response to that challenge they will be judged. When he calls men to follow him, he takes it for granted that they will obey, recognizing that he has the authority to command. To one young man he gave the command to sell all that he had, to take up the cross and follow the Master (Mark 10: 21). This took place at a particular crisis of his ministry, at which any half-heartedness would be fatal. Nor is the command to sell all to be generalized, as though it was literally to be fulfilled by anyone who wished to follow Jesus. But in principle the command is the same for all—not to be good or to keep the commandments, but to hear the call of the one whose challenge is so severe and so inescapable.

CHAPTER SEVEN

HOW CAN WE THINK OF JESUS TODAY?

How can a man who lived nineteen centuries ago be of any use to me, a man of the 1970s, engaged in living out my life in the circumstances of the twentieth century?

This is a real problem for many men of goodwill who would like to be Christians. They are baffled by history. If we try to catch Jesus as he was in the days of the Gospels, he seems all the time to slip through our fingers. If we try to make him real to ourselves today, are we really doing more than glorifying our own imaginations, and calling these Jesus of Nazareth, when we might in reality just as well call them Buddha or Sinbad the sailor?

This dilemma has sometimes been expressed as the contrast between the Jesus of history and the Christ of faith, and the difficulty of bringing them together into any kind of a unity.

Up to a point we can admit the appropriateness of the phrase. The resurrection of Jesus does mark a dividing line; the faith of the Church after it was in many ways different from the stumbling faith of the disciples before it. We cannot think the resurrection away. A number of modern writers have tried to write lives of Jesus from which the supernatural is entirely excluded, and only that which can be accepted as "historical" is allowed to remain. Some of these portraits are attractive; but on the whole they are rather insipid and commonplace, and that means that they are not in the least like Jesus as he is depicted in all our sources and in all our traditions. He is always a strange and challenging personality. If we wish to sum up in a few words the kind of impression that he made on those who saw him, we cannot do better than take Mark 10:32: "And they were on the road going up to Jerusalem; and Jesus was walking ahead of them; and they were amazed; and those who followed were afraid." The terms express not human fear, but overpowering religious awe. However limited our understanding of him, the Jesus of history and the Christ of faith are one.

Groups which believed in the resurrection used all kinds of terms and titles to give expression to their new-found faith. But never for a single moment did they forget that the object of their veneration was a carpenter who had lived in quite recent times in Galilee. The figure of a crucified Jew was never lost sight of in the glory of a divine manifestation. It was Jesus whom they proclaimed as Lord. They fixed him firmly in history and not in fiction, by declaring in the clause which very early became a part of the Christian creed, that he was "crucified under Pontius Pilate".

If we wish to stress this point still further, we shall find notable support for it in the narratives of the resurrection in the Gospels. Among the various points that are common to all the various stories, one is particularly relevant here. The disciples had difficulty in recognizing the risen Lord; but, once they had recognized him, they found that he was the same Master whom they had known before his death, and that the fellowship they now had with him was the same that it had always been, except that now it was always available and uninterrupted by the circumstances of time and distance. It was into this fellowship with the risen Jesus that they called the new believers.

Moreover, it is a mistake to treat Jesus as an isolated phenomenon, and to separate him from his background in the Old Testament. The Old Testament is not like the sacred books of any other ancient religion. It introduces us to a God who is the living God, a God who calls and chooses a people and guides their destiny through all the changes and chances of history, a God whose concern is for righteousness, and who chooses mercy rather than sacrifice (Hos. 6: 6; Matt. 9: 13; 12: 7). All this Jesus could assume; when he spoke he was not speaking into a vacuum, but into the minds of men and women who had been prepared by these ancient Scriptures to accept his message.

One group failed to detach Jesus sufficiently from that Old Testament background. To use one of his own striking phrases, he was like "a householder, who brings out of his treasure what is new and what is old" (Matt. 13: 52). Those who failed to apprehend all that was new in the message of Jesus would have kept him imprisoned in the past, as the founder of a new sect of Judaism. But for that kind of Judaeo-Christianity there really was no future; within a comparatively short time it died out and exercised no further influence on Christian history.

At the other extreme was a group which would have liked to detach Jesus completely from his Old Testament origins. The second century heretic Marcion believed that the God of the Old Testament, the God of the Jews, could not be the same as the loving God who was manifested in Jesus of Nazareth. His Bible, therefore, would have contained no Old Testament at all. The Church refused to accept this argument. It did not always know what to do with the Old Testament; but it affirmed that Jesus could rightly be understood only in the light of a purpose which reached back through prophets and patriarchs to the creation of the world, and which would reach forward to the consummation of which the prophets of old had spoken.

This is the framework into which Jesus fits. To say that he was a historical figure means to accept the fact that he was born at a particular time and place, spoke a particular language as his own, was conditioned at every point by the type of civilization in which he had grown up, and in many things shared the ideas of his contemporaries. This means that to us men of the twentieth century the Gospels are at many points perplexing books. We cannot always be certain that we catch all the inflections of the voice of Jesus, all the subtle overtones and undertones of his utterance.

But to say that Jesus fits exactly into one historical setting and into the framework of one already existing religion is by no means to say that he is provincial and of limited significance. The particular is often also the universal. Socrates could not possibly have been anyone but an Athenian philosopher, but we are still glad to go to school with him today. So Jesus was a Jew living in the early days of the Roman Empire. But to a quite astonishing extent his words and his actions are free from the limitations of his time; they are not "situation-conditioned" but are of universal significance.

The words and actions of Jesus cannot be neatly separated from one another. In action no less than in word he was showing what the Kingdom of God is, and what demands it makes upon the sons of men. But from his words and actions together it should be possible to work out certain principles by which he ruled his own life, and to infer from these the way in which he understood the world and which he commended for acceptance by his friends:

1. The ultimate reality of this universe, in spite of appearances, is not material but spiritual. In the Fourth Gospel Jesus is represented as affirming that God is spirit (John 4: 24). In the other three Gospels the word "Spirit" is rarely used; but the principle is everywhere present—there are things that matter more than food and raiment (Matt. 6: 24–34).

2. Whatever appearances may suggest, the invisible power behind the phenomena of the world is beneficent and cares for men. He makes his sun to rise on the evil and on the good, and sends rain on the just and the unjust. (Matt. 5: 45). He is

78

kind to the unthankful and to the evil (Luke 6: 35). For this reason it is important not to forget that those who are rejected by men may be the very ones who are accepted by the heavenly Father.

3. This unseen power is not remote from men. He is so intimately involved in their concerns that it can be said that not a sparrow falls to the ground without his knowledge (Luke 12: 6-7). But this means also that men can speak with him, and that the prayer of the sinner who says "God be merciful to me" will not be rejected (Luke 18: 13).

4. God calls men to work with him. He is like a man who sends out labourers into his vineyard (Matt. 20: 1-16). All the prophets and wise men have been his servants, carrying out his work in their day. Now he has chosen one to be his servant, his son in a special way; and this Son too calls men with authority into the service of the kingdom.

5. Those who are called need not at the start be good in the sense of "virtuous". What is required is that they shall be wholly committed to the cause to which they have set their hand—there is to be no withdrawal, no putting the hand to the plough and then looking back (Luke 9: 57-62). But this total commitment means the end of all earthly vanity and ambition. It is the natural ambition of men to get to the top of the tree; those who would serve the kingdom must be prepared to take the lowest place and to make themselves the servants of all (Luke 14: 7-11; 22: 24-27).

6. To choose the service of the kingdom is necessarily to choose the way of suffering. The kingdoms of men are organized on entirely different principles. Men are certain to resent the kind of radical challenge which must be presented by Jesus and his followers; and, if the challenge is pushed home, they will defend themselves against it by destroying those through whom the challenge is presented. It has always been so. Israel has always killed those whom God has sent to

him. Jesus takes it for granted that the presentation of his message at the heart and centre of the Jewish religion in Jerusalem will be followed by his death. This is one of the hazards of being a prophet. Nor does he hold out to his disciples any other expectation. They will bring a message of joy, and will try to make themselves the servants of all; their names will be cast out as evil, just as was the name of their Master (Matt. 5: 11–12).

7. But this is not the last word. Man can kill; it rests with God to make alive. It is hard to say exactly how Jesus foresaw his own resurrection. We shall do well to think of his foreknowledge not as a magical revelation of the future, but as a deep insight into the very nature of things. God's cause must go forward to victory. The death of the messenger has come to be seen as a necessary part of the progress of that cause; it will not be strange if the messenger also is caught up into the triumph and is vindicated by the God in whose name he has done all that he has done. God is not the God of the dead but of the living (Luke 20: 38); those who believe will sit down with Abraham, Isaac and Jacob in the kingdom of heaven (Matt. 8: 11).

That is the way in which Jesus lived. Those whom he called he called to the adventure of learning to live as he lived. In essence the situation has not changed; that is still the challenge that he presents today.

In one way everything has been changed. The resurrection has taken place; Jesus has been vindicated, and the decisive battle between the forces of good and evil has been won. But the victory is still a hidden reality, evident to the eyes of faith alone. The world, as even the Christian sees it, is still a place of intense conflict, in which the powers of evil are still immensely strong.

To accept the call of Christ is no easy option. It does not allow a man to contract out of the business of living into some supposedly holier world from which sin and conflict have been excluded. It commits him to living in the world, but in uncompromising loyalty to the good as he has seen it in Christ, and in persistent hostility to all those disorders in men and in society which led to the crucifixion of Jesus Christ, and would almost certainly cause him to be crucified again, if he were alive on earth today.

Anyone who tries to follow Christ in this way cannot go far without becoming aware of his own unfitness to be engaged in this campaign. He is dismayed to find that to a large extent his own outlook and actions are determined by those very powers of evil that he is pledged to fight. The battle is within him and outside. It is at this point that the doctrine of forgiveness as set forth in Jesus comes to his rescue. Jesus was the friend of sinners, of the outcast and the rejected. He did not receive them because they were acceptable. He accepted them because of what he saw that they could become through the power of his acceptance.

The follower of Jesus, like the Master before him, accepts himself in the situation in which he has been placed—as living in one century and not another, as a citizen of one country and not of another, as speaking one language and not another. But he is never wholly identified with that situation and never wholly acquiescent in it. Jesus was a Jew, yet he was the most radical critic of what Judaism had become, just because men had put a system in the place of the living God, and had allowed their traditions to make his word of none effect (Mark 7: 9–13). The follower of Jesus will always be something of a revolutionary; he will always be suspicious of systems, and even of the system of the Church since that can so easily become the prison-house and not the dwelling-place of the Spirit of God.

The Christian will not be buoyed up by an airy optimism, as though the Kingdom of God could quickly and easily come among men. But he will not yield to the pessimistic idea that nothing can be done. There is no final victory this side of the coming of Christ to wind up the whole process of history. But there are innumerable partial victories to be won. Jesus was killed, but the Church survived to be and to remain the great creative power in the life of men.

Just because Jesus left so few detailed rules the man who is trying to serve him has no ready book of reference, not even the Gospels, to which he can turn to find instructions for action in all situations. This means that he must constantly turn back from the written sources to the Source from which all things come, in an attitude of attentive and expectant listening. But here he finds that he is doing exactly what Jesus of Nazareth did; his whole life was one continuous and unbroken dialogue with his heavenly Father. He was not endowed with any magical means of communication. He, like any other man, had to set aside times for listening, to enquire, to explore, to discern for himself exactly what God's Will might be. Because his own will was perfectly geared to the Will of God, he made no mistakes—he knew where to go, and when to act, and what to say.

The follower of Jesus has no guarantee of infallibility. He is liable to be distracted by human considerations, to shrink from what is difficult, to mistake his own predilections for divine aims. But all the time he has in the record of Jesus of Nazareth an objective standard, by which all things can be tested, the spurious shown up for what it is, the genuine distinguished from the counterfeit. The Christian, developing the habit of turning a hundred times a day to consider in every situation what the Will of God may be, finds that his life too is growing into the pattern of an unbroken dialogue with God.

He makes a further interesting discovery. The word "God" has come to be filled with entirely new content and significance. Everyone supposes himself to know what the word "God" means; but in fact the word is simply an empty vessel into which content has to be poured. The Christian finds that he can never think of God without thinking of Jesus Christ, and that he can never think of Jesus Christ without thinking of God. This has nothing directly to do with the theological doctrine of the Trinity, though it probably helped to prepare the way for it in Christian experience. It is simply that even the Old Testament idea of God, magnificent as it is, no longer covers the Christian's experience and has had to be radically transformed. Vast new dimensions have been added by the death of Jesus Christ for man's redemption, seen now as God's own decisive act, God's willingness himself to enter to the utmost into the chaos and tragedy brought about by human sin, and to bring victory out of the depths of apparently total defeat. Another dimension has been added by the awareness that Jesus is "the same yesterday, today, and for ever" (Heb. 13:5). To "remember" him in the celebration of the Lord's Supper is not to think with sorrow or gratitude of a long-departed friend; it is to relive with him, as a present reality, the experiences of the Upper Room, of Gethsemane, of Golgotha, of Easter morning, and so to become aware of him as the present Master of the feast.

Throughout this book we have recognized the part that has been played by interpretation in the development of the Gospels as we have them, and in the picture that they present to us of Jesus Christ. Many students of the Gospel, even conservative students, would be inclined to think that the last three verses of Matthew's Gospel record not so much words actually spoken by Jesus Christ, as a summary of what the Church had come to believe, in the light of the resurrection, to be his will and purpose for his Church. But, if so, how did they arrive at this formulation, and what did they mean by the words that they used?

Why did they claim that "all authority in heaven and on earth has been given to me"? Simply because, having lived in that faith, they had come to know that "all things are possible to him who believes" (Mark 9: 23), and that the name of Jesus is the power that restores life and gives triumph over death.

Why did they write "Go ye therefore, and make disciples of all nations"? Because they had come to see that the death and resurrection of Jesus Christ are of significance to everyone living upon the earth, and that to fail to make these tidings known is to rob man of the most important part of his inheritance as man.

Why did they write, "Lo, I am with you always, to the close of the age"? Because this was their astonishing experience in the days that followed the resurrection. Before his death, Jesus had sent the disciples out on mission; they had had the experience of being separated from him, and of returning to him to report. Once they had come to believe in the realiy of the resurrection, they found that there was no more coming or going, but only one perpetual presence; he was always there.

If these words had not been written in Matthew's Gospel, any follower of Christ would have been able to construct them out of his own experience and in his own words. Jesus is always

The indwelling and inspiring power,
The unending theme of proclamation,
The creator of the fellowship of believers,
The one whose presence brings unutterable joy,
The one who guarantees the final triumph of his cause,
The one who stands at the end of the world to welcome the traveller home.

Jesus can be all these things today because he was all these things in the days of his life in Galilee and Judaea. Some things were much clearer after the resurrection than they had been before; but they could become clear only because they were implicit not in this saying or that act, but in the whole of what he said and did and was.